LiFE SCIENCE DAYBOOK

In Collaboration with NSTA

GREaT SoURCe
EDUCATION GROUP
A Houghton Mifflin Company

Acknowledgments

Reviewers

Barbara Oechslin Clark
Jefferson County Public Schools
Louisville, Kentucky

Bonnie Hayes
Golden, Colorado

Terry L. Johnson
Springville, Utah

Dr. Louise Moulding
Davis School District
Farmington, Utah

Dwight D. Sieggreen
Northville Public Schools
Northville, Michigan

Juliana Texley
Central Michigan University
New Baltimore, Michigan

Credits

Writing: Bill Smith Studio

Editorial: Great Source: Fran Needham, Marianne Knowles, Susan Rogalski; Bill Smith Studio

Design: Great Source: Richard Spencer; Bill Smith Studio

Production Management: Great Source: Evelyn Curley; Bill Smith Studio

Cover Design: Bill Smith Studio

National Science Teachers Association: Tyson Brown, Carol Duval, Juliana Texley, Patricia Warren, Stephen J. Farenga

Photos

Page 4: PhotoDisc; **5:** PhotoDisc; **6–7:** Corel; **8:** PhotoDisc; **9:** Corbis/Royalty Free; **12–13:** PhotoDisc; **15:** Painet, Inc.; **16–17:** Painet, Inc.; **17:** ©J. Bavosi/Photo Researchers, Inc.; **18–19:** PhotoDisc; **21:** © K. Porter/Photo Researchers, Inc.; **22–23:** PhotoDisc; **24:** PhotoDisc; **26–27:** PhotoDisc; **28–29:** PhotoDisc; **30:** © G. Murti/Photo Researchers, Inc.; **33:** PhotoDisc; **35:** © Claude Edelmann/Photo Researchers, Inc.; **36–37:** PhotoDisc; **39:** © Keith Porter/Photo Researchers, Inc.; **40:** ©Dr. Neal Scolding/Photo Researchers, Inc. ; **42–43:** ArtToday; **44:** NASA; **46–47:** Bill Smith Studio art; **48:** PhotoDisc; **50:** Digital Vision; **51:** PhotoDisc; **53:** PhotoDisc; **54:** PhotoDisc; **56–57:** Corel; **58:** PhotoSpin; **58–59:** PhotoDisc; **60–61:** PhotoDisc; **62:** Hutchings Photography; **64–65:** PhotoDisc; **65:** © Kevin Fugate; **66–67:** Bill Smith Studio art; **68–69:** PhotoDisc; **70–71:** © Biophoto Associates/Photo Researchers, Inc.; **72:** Corel; **74a:** PhotoDisc; **74b:** © Joe McDonald/CORBIS; **076:** Corel; **77:** © AFP/CORBIS; **78:** ; **78–79:** Bill Smith Studio art; **80:** PhotoDisc, Corel, PhotoDisc; **81a:** PhotoDisc; **81b:** © D Suzio/Photo Researchers, Inc. ; **82:** PhotoSpin; **83:** ©STR/Reuters/TimePix; **84–85:** PhotoDisc; **84a:** ©STR/Reuters/TimePix; **84b:** PhotoDisc; **84c:** PhotoDisc; **84d:** Corel; **86–87:** Corbis; **87a:** Corel; **87b:** ArtToday; **87c:** Corel; **87d:** ArtToday; **88–89:** Bill Smith Studio art; **90:** Corel; **92:** PhotoDisc; **93:** Corel; **94a:** PhotoDisc ; **94b:** PhotoDisc; **95:** PhotoDisc; **96–97:** PhotoDisc; **98:** ©Oliver Meckes/Nicole Ottawa/Photo Researchers, Inc.; **99:** Painet, Inc.; **100:** PhotoDisc; **100–101:** Bill Smith Studio art; **101:** ©Bettmann/Corbis; **102:** ©Scimat/Photo Researchers, Inc.; **104:** ©L. West/Photo Researchers, Inc.; **105:** Corel; **107a:** Corel; **107b:** ©N. Poritz/Photo Researchers, Inc.; **107c:** Corel; **108a:** ©S. Dalton/Photo Researchers, Inc.; **108b:** ©S. Dalton/Photo Researchers, Inc.; **109:** Corel; **110:** Corel; **111:** © John Mitchell/Photo Researchers,Inc.; **114:** © Tom Brakefield/CORBIS; **116–117:** Painet, Inc.; **119:** Corel; **120–121:** Corel; **122:** © Stuart Westmorland/CORBIS; **123a:** Corel; **123b:** © Kennan Ward/CORBIS; **123c:** corel; **124:** Ron Leighton; **125:** ©Peter Slater/Photo Researchers Inc.; **128:** PhotoDisc; **130a:** PhotoDisc; **130b:** © Sally A. Morgan;Ecoscene/CORBIS; **131:** ©Nuridsany et Perennou/Photo Researchers, Inc. ; **132:** Corel; **134:** © Nathan Blow/AllSport; **135:** Zigy Kaluzny/Stone; **136:** PhotoDisc; **137:** Hutchings Photography; **138–139:** PhotoDisc; **140:** Hutchings Photography; **141:** Corel; **142:** Corel; **143:** Hutchings Photography; **144:** PhotoDisc; **146:** Corel; **147:** © Susan Leavines/Photo Researchers; **148–149:** ArtToday; **150:** PhotoDisc; **151:** © Doug Martin/Photo Researchers, Inc.; **152–153:** Bill Smith Studio art; **154:** Corel; **155:** Corel; **156:** PhotoDisc; **157:** Courtesy of Marcus E. Raichle, M.D.; Washington University School of : Medicine; **159:** PhotoDisc; **160–161:** © A Hobson/Photo Resarchers, Inc.; **163:** PhotoDisc; **164–165:** PhotoDisc; **166:** ©Biophoto Associates/Photo Researchers, Inc.; **167:** ©Bettmann/Corbis ; **168–169:** ©Bettmann/CORBIS; **169:** Bettmann/Corbis; **169:** ©Bettmann/Corbis; **171:** ©S. Stammers/Photo Researchers, Inc.; **172:** ©Getty Images; **173:** PhotoDisc; **174:** PhotoDisc; **178:** ©Galen Rowell/Corbis; **182:** ©Frank Lane Picture Agency/Corbis; **184:** PhotoDisc; **188:** Corel ; **189:** Corel; **191:** Corel; **193:** Corel; **195:** Corel; **196–197:** Corel; **198:** PhotoDisc; **199:** Corel; **200–201:** Corel; **204–205:** PhotoDisc; **209:** Corel; **210–211:** Corel; **213:** PhotoDisc; **214:** PhotoDisc; **216–217:** PhotoDisc

Cover: All images PhotoDisc

Illustration: Thomas Gagliano

Printed in the United States of America.
International Standard Book Number: 0-669-49246-9
2 3 4 5 6 7 8 9 10 — DBH — 10 09 08 07 06 05 04 03

Sources

10, 34 Hoagland, Mahlon, and Bert Dodson. *The Way Life Works: Everything You Need to Know About the Way All Life Grows, Develops, Reproduces, and Gets Along.* Reprinted by permission of Times Books, a division of Random House, Inc.

14 Shroyer, Jo Ann. *Quarks, Critters, and Chaos: What Science Terms Really Mean.* Prentice Hall General Reference. Reprinted by permission of the author.

18 "Clones: Double Trouble?" *TIME* for Kids. TIME Inc. (www.timeforkids.com/TFK/magazines/story/0,6277,93229,00.html). Used with permission of *TIME for Kids* magazine, 2002.

20 Excerpt from A WIND IN THE DOOR by Madeline L'Engle. Copyright ©1973 by Crosswicks, Ltd. Reprinted by permission of Farrar, Straus, & Giroux, LLC.

24 Netting, Jessica. "Gene Found For Chloroplast Movement." *Science News.* Reprinted with permission from SCIENCE NEWS, the weekly newsmagazine of science, copyright 2001 by Science Service Inc.

28, 38, 142 Reprinted by permission of *MadSci Network.* Washington University Medical School. (www.madsci.org)

30 Baeurele, Patrick and Norbert Landa. *The Cell Works: An Expedition Into the Fantastic World of Cells.* Reprinted by permission of Barron's Education Series, Inc.

40 "The BIG Questions." *Ask Dr. Universe,* sponsored by Washington State University. (www.wsu.edu/DrUniverse/body.html) Reprinted by permission of the author.

44 "Scientists Grow Heart Tissue In Bioreactor." Reprinted by permission of *Science@NASA.* NASA. (science.nasa.gov/newhome/headlines/msad05oct99_1.htm)

48 "Thyroid Disorders." *KidsHealth.* Reprinted by permission of The Nemours Foundation. (kidshealth.org/kid/health_problems/gland/thyroid.html)

52 Ridley, Matt. Genome: The Autobiography of a Species in 23 Chapters. Reprinted by permission of HarperCollins Publishers, Inc.

54 Henig, Robin Marantz. *The Monk in the Garden.* Reprinted by permission of Houghton Mifflin.

58 from THEY CAME FROM DNA by Bill Aronson, 1993 by Billy Aronson. Reprinted by permission of Henry Holt and Company, LLC.

64 Trost, Cathy. "The Blue People of Troublesome Creek." *Science 82.* Reprinted by permission of the author.

68 "Our Genetic Identity." American Museum of Natural History from the exhibit "The Genomic Revolution." (www.amnh.org/exhibitions/genomics/1_identity/nature.html)

72 Wollard, Kathy. "The Long and Short of Giraffes." *Newsday,* August 11, 1998.

76 "Poaching Creates Tuskless Elephants." Reprinted by permission of United Press International, June 19, 2001.

82 Trevedi, Bijal P. "New Insect Order Found in Southern Africa." *National Geographic Today.* National Geographic Channel – US, all rights reserved.

86 "Giant Panda." (www.nature.ca/notebooks/english/gpanda.htm) Illustration by Charles Douglas. Reprinted by permission of the Canadian Museum of Nature.

94 Netting, Jessica. "Dirty Money Harbors Bacterial Dangers." Science News. Reprinted with permission from SCIENCE NEWS, the weekly newsmagazine of science, copyright 2001 by Science Service Inc.

98 Moore, Pete. *Killer Germs: Rogue Diseases of the Twenty–First Century.* Reprinted by permission of Carlton Books Limited 2001.

102 "Bacteria" essay excerpt by Rachel Mock, Young Naturalist Awards 1998 winner. The Young Naturalist Awards is a program of the American Museum of Natural History. http://www.amnh.org/nationalcenter/youngnaturalistawards/1998/bacteria.html

104, 108 Text by Matthew Robertson from *Pathfinders: Insects and Spiders* ©Weldon Own Pty Ltd.

110 Pringle, Laurence. *A Dragon in the Sky: The Story of a Green Darner Dragonfly.* Reprinted by permission of Orchard Books, a Division of Scholastic, Inc.

114 Ford, John K.B., Graeme M. Ellis, and Kenneth C. Balcomb. *Killer Whales.* Reprinted by permission of University of British Columbia Press. Second Edition. 2000.

118, 122 Ford, John K.B., Graeme M. Ellis. *Transients: Mammal–Hunting Killer Whales.* Reprinted by permission of University of British Columbia Press 1999.

124, 128 Kneidel, Sally. *Skunk Cabbage, Sundew Plants & Strangler Figs: And 18 More Of The Strangest Plants On Earth.* 2001 John Wiley & Sons, Inc. This material is used by permission of John Wiley & Sons, Inc. ©2001

136 Raloff, Janet. "Surprise! Fat Proves A Taste Sensation." *Science News.* Reprinted with permission from SCIENCE NEWS, the weekly newsmagazine of science, copyright 2001 by Science Service Inc.

140 Reprinted with the permission of Simon & Schuster Books for Young Readers, an imprint of Simon & Schuster Children's Publishing Division from YIKES! YOUR BODY, UP CLOSE by Mike Janulewicz. Copyright ©1997 The Templar Company Plc.

146 "Your Digestive System and How it Works." *National Digestive Diseases Information Clearinghouse.* Reprinted by permission of the National Institutes of Health. (www.niddk.nih.gov/health/digest/pubs/digesyst/newdiges.htm)

150 "Amazing Heart Facts." From "NOVA" at www.pbs.org/wgbh/nova/heart/heartfacts.html Copyright ©2002 WGBH/Boston.

154 "Muscles and Bones; Einstein; Stars Chat; Raptor Center." *Newton's Apple.* Reprinted by permission of KTCA. (www.pbs.org/ktca/newtons/newtonsclassics/classic11.html)

156 Barnes, Kate, and Steve Weston. *How It Works: The Human Body.* Barnes & Noble Books. Reprinted by permission of Award Publications.

158 "The Teenage Brain: Why Do We Sleep?" PBS: The Secret Life of the Brain. Public Broadcasting System. (http://www.pbs.org/wnet/brain/episode3/sleep/2.html)

162 Text: Whitfield, Philip, ed. *The Human Body Explained: A Guide to Understanding the Incredible Living Machine.* Henry Holt and Company, 1995. Reprinted by permission of Marshall Editions. Illustration: *Visual Magic,* p. 39. Reprinted by permission from Breslich & Foss Limited.

166 Reprinted with the permission of Atheneum Books for Young Readers, an imprint of Simon & Schuster Children's Publishing Division from GREAT LIVES: MEDICINE by Robert H. Curtis, M.D. Copyright 1993 Robert H. Curtis.

170 Copyright 1999 *Epidemic!: The World of Infectious Disease* edited by Rob Desalle. Reprinted by permission of The New Press. (800) 233 4830.

172 "Facts About Infectious Diseases." Reprinted by permission of the Centers for Disease Control and Prevention. United States Department of Health and Human Services. (www.cdc.gov/ncidod/op/materials/opbrochure.PDF)

178 "The Unwanted Amphibian." *Frog Decline Reversal Project.* Reprinted by permission of the Frog Decline Reversal Project, Inc. (www.fdrproject.org/pages/TDprogress.htm)

182 "Cane Toads—Bufo Marinus." *Australian Museum Fact Sheets.* Reprinted by permission of Australian Museum. (www.amonline.net.au/factsheets/canetoad.htm)

186 Schulz, Dennis. "The Cane Toad Dialogues: Disaster or Disruption?" from *Savanna Links,* Issue 16, October–December 2000. Reprinted by permission of the Tropical Savannas Cooperative Research Centre. Northern Territory University. (savanna.ntu.edu.au/publications/savanna_links16/toad.html)

188, 192, 196 Bock, Carl E., and Jane H. Bock. *The View from Bald Hill: Thirty Years in an Arizona Grassland.* Reprinted by permission of University of California Press.

198, 202 Medici, Patricia, and J. Pablo Juliá. "Scientists Trap, Tag, And Track Tapirs To Design A Survival Strategy." *Eco–Exchange.* October–November 2001. Reprinted by permission of the Rainforest Alliance. (ra.org/programs/cmc/newsletter/nov01–2.html)

208 Diamond, Jared. "Easter's End." *Discover.* Reprinted by permission of the publisher and author.

212 The text was excerpted from the JASON Academy Course Human Impacts 101, Aquatic Ecology. For more information on online courses, go to www.jason.org/Academy(http://www.jason.org/Academy). Reynolds, Karen. "Human Impacts 101." (www.nsta.org/361/)

214 Pringle, Laurence. *Living Treasure: Saving Earth's Threatened Biodiversity.* HarperCollins Children's Books. Reprinted by permission of the author.

Chapter 1
STRUCTURE OF
A CELL

1 **Sentries at the Gate** *The cell membrane controls what goes into and out of the cell.* 10

2 **All Kinds of Parts** *The cell is made up of many organelles.* 14

3 **The Nucleus and DNA** *The nucleus controls the functioning of the cell's other organelles.* 18

Chapter 2
CELLS AT
WORK

4 **Energy for Life** *During cellular respiration, mitochondria release energy by breaking down glucose.* 20

5 **Photosynthesis** *During photosynthesis, plant cells change carbon dioxide and water into glucose.* 24

6 **All Together Now** *Cellular respiration and photosynthesis are complementary processes.* 28

Chapter 3
CELL DIVISION

7 **One Becomes Two** *During mitosis, a cell divides to produce two daughter cells, each with the same number of chromosomes as the parent cell.* 30

8 **The Sorcerer's Apprentice** *Cell growth is exponential.* 34

9 **Cells Out of Control** *Cancer is cell division out of control.* 38

Chapter 4
WHEN CELLS
GET TOGETHER

10 **All Charged Up** *Cells use electricity to communicate.* 40

11 **Growing Tissue** *Scientists have found a way to grow tissue from an adult's stem cells.* 44

12 **Organ Misfire** *When an organ is not functioning normally, other organs are affected.* 48

UNIT 2 Heredity, Diversity, and Change   50

Chapter 5
HOW GENES WORK

13 **Your Genes and Chromosomes** *DNA contains the instructions for all of an organism's physical traits.*   52

14 **In-gene-ius!** *Gregor Mendel investigated inherited traits in pea plants.*   54

15 **Custom Corn** *Selective breeding produces organisms with desirable traits.*   58

Chapter 6
GENES AND PEOPLE

16 **Single-Gene Human Traits** *Some human physical traits are controlled by a single gene.*   62

17 **The Blue People of Kentucky** *Blue-tinged skin is caused by the recessive form of a gene.*   64

18 **More Than Just Genes** *Genes alone do not determine all of a person's characteristics.*   68

Chapter 7
MOST LIKELY TO SURVIVE

19 **The Right Stuff** *Adaptations enable a species to survive in its environment.*   72

20 **Tall, Gray, and Tuskless** *In some populations of Asian elephants, the gene for growing tusks is being lost due to illegal hunting.*   76

21 **New and Improved** *Adaptive radiation and convergent evolution are two results of natural selection.*   80

Chapter 8
ONE HUNDRED MILLION KINDS OF THINGS

22 **What's in a Name?** *When scientists discover a new organism, they must determine how it fits into the scientific classification system.*   82

23 **We Are Family** *Organisms are sometimes reclassified based on new evidence.*   86

24 **It's Classified!** *A dichotomous key helps identify organisms by presenting a series of choices.*   90

UNIT 3 Living Things   92

Chapter 9
BACTERIA

25 **More Bacteria for Your Buck** *Bacteria thrive on paper money.*   94

26 **The Bad Guys** *Some bacteria are deadly.*   98

27 **Bacteria at Work** *Some bacteria help keep us healthy.*   102

Chapter 10
HOW INSECTS GET AROUND

28 **Walk Like an Insect** *An insect's body structure makes it stable as it walks.* 104

29 **Jump!** *Structures for jumping help insects survive.* 108

30 **Flights of Fancy** *Flying and migration are structural and behavioral adaptations of some insects.* 110

Chapter 11
KILLER WHALES: WOLVES OF THE SEA

31 **Sounds of the Sea** *Killer whales use sound to navigate and to communicate under water.* 114

32 **The Hunters** *Killer whales show cooperative behavior when hunting.* 118

33 **Name That Whale** *Marine biologists use a system to identify individual killer whales.* 122

Chapter 12
PLANT ADAPTATIONS

34 **Mistletoe, Birds, and Trees** *Mistletoe plants depend on symbiotic relationships with other organisms to survive.* 124

35 **Not Your Usual Carnivores** *Some plants have adaptations that enable them to capture and consume insects.* 128

36 **What Attracts Insects to Flowers?** *Flowers have features that attract insects.* 132

UNIT 4 Human Body Systems

134

Chapter 13
COMING TO OUR SENSES

37 **Testing Taste Buds** *Scientists are investigating whether humans can taste fat.* 136

38 **Balancing Act** *Our inner ears help us maintain balance.* 140

39 **How Does It Feel?** *Our sense of touch provides important information about our environment.* 142

Chapter 14
BODY WORK

40 **In One End...** *The digestive system breaks down food and absorbs nutrients.* 146

41 **The Beat Goes On** *The health of the circulatory system is affected by diet and behavior.* 150

42 **On the Move** *The human body has three types of muscle tissue: skeletal muscle, cardiac muscle, and smooth muscle.* 154

Chapter 15
A MIND OF ITS OWN

43 **Brain Scan** *Different parts of the brain do different things.* 156

44 **Sleep On It** *Sleep may play an important role in learning.* 158

45 **Seeing Things** *The brain interprets what the eye sees.* 162

Chapter 16
DISEASES THROUGH TIME

46 **Conquering Polio** *Vaccines help the body's immune system fight the viruses that cause polio.*   166

47 **The Buzz on Malaria** *Malaria is an infectious disease that continues to plague the world today.*   170

48 **Help Yourself Stay Healthy** *Infectious diseases can be prevented.*   172

UNIT 5 Ecology   176

Chapter 17
POPULATIONS, COMMUNITIES, AND ECOSYSTEMS

49 **The Cane Toad Invasion** *Cane toad populations in Australia have grown at an alarming rate.*   178

50 **Poison Toads** *A cane toad population interacts with other populations in its community.*   182

51 **Bad Neighbors** *Cane toad populations affect their entire ecosystem.*   186

Chapter 18
UNDER THE GRASSLAND SKY

52 **Eat or Be Eaten** *Coyotes and rodents illustrate predator-prey feeding relationships in a desert ecosystem.*   188

53 **A Place of Their Own** *Different species can survive in the same ecosystem by occupying different habitats.*   192

54 **The Fragile Land** *Humans often make changes that affect ecosystems.*   196

Chapter 19
RAIN FOREST

55 **Let It Rain** *The tapir's structural adaptations enable it to survive in its tropical rain forest ecosystem.*   198

56 **The Seeds of Biodiversity** *Tapirs serve an important role in maintaining the biodiversity of the tropical rain forest.*   202

57 **Going, Going... Gone?** *If the deforestation of tropical rain forests is not slowed, one of Earth's most valuable ecosystems will be destroyed.*   206

Chapter 20
PROTECTING EARTH

58 **The Lesson of Easter Island** *The earliest civilization on Easter Island destroyed the island's natural resources.*   208

59 **People Make a Difference** *Human population growth has a direct impact on aquatic ecosystems.*   212

60 **Be an Eco-Hero** *Biodiversity can be found in even a small plot of land.*   214

Glossary   218

Cells

Do you know why cells are called "cells"?

The first person to observe cells was an English scientist named Robert Hooke. In 1665, Hooke looked at a piece of cork using a microscope and drew a comparison between what he saw and something he was already familiar with. He thought that the sections making up the cork looked like the rooms that monks lived in, which are called "cells." Hooke decided to call the cork sections "cells," too.

In this unit, you will learn all about cells, the small but complex building blocks of all living things. Cells carry out all the activities that keep a living thing alive. For example, they take in nutrients, water, and air. They get rid of wastes, use energy, grow, and reproduce themselves. You'll also learn how cells join together to form tissues, organs, and organ systems. Finally, you'll learn what can happen when cells stop functioning normally.

THE CHAPTERS IN
THIS UNIT ARE . . .

CHAPTER 1:
Structure of a Cell
Find Out: How is a cell membrane like a herd of musk oxen?

CHAPTER 2:
Cells at Work
Find Out: Why do chloroplasts in a leaf move around?

CHAPTER 3:
Cell Division
Find Out: How does cancer start?

CHAPTER 4:
When Cells Get Together
Find Out: How much electricity do the cells in your body generate?

? DID YOU KNOW?
Your body is made of trillions of cells. Almost 300,000,000 of them die every minute!

Structure of a Cell

Sentries at the Gate

There are many structures inside a cell. What keeps the structures inside the cell and keeps out things that can damage those important structures? The cell membrane.

Your body contains billions of cells! Cells are the building blocks of life. Some organisms are made up of only one cell, while others are made up of millions of cells. Imagine that your fingertip is the size of a room and the room is filled with rice grains. Each grain would represent one cell. Can you imagine the number of cells in your fingertip?

Cells are filled with a fluid called cytoplasm. A thin membrane surrounds every cell. This membrane forms a boundary between the inside of the cell and its surroundings.

▶ **Before You Read**

THINK ABOUT IT Boundaries keep things in and out. For example, a fence marks the boundary of a yard. The fence also keeps the pet dog and the young children in. It keeps strange dogs and bicyclists out.

▶ *Think about the boundaries in your environment. Name five boundaries that you can see around you. For each one, tell what marks the boundary. List what is kept in and what is kept out by the boundary.*

_____

_____

_____

_____

_____

_____

_____

_____

> ▶ **Read**

It can be easier to understand something new by comparing it with something else.

Heads Out—Tails In

When danger threatens, musk oxen gather in a circle—heads and horns to the outside, tails to the inside—sheltering their calves in the center. This circle of protection illustrates one of life's organizing principles—a difference between in and out. Life's chemicals need to be kept close together so that they can meet and react readily. The inner environment needs a saltiness, acidity, temperature, etc., different from the outside. These differences are maintained by some form of protective barrier, such as a baby's skin, a clam's shell, or a cell's membrane.

The membrane surrounding each of our cells behaves something like the threatened musk oxen. The fat molecules that make up the membrane have a water-liking head and a fat-liking tail. Heads face outside toward the watery environment beyond the cell; tails face inward. Since the inside of a cell also has a watery environment, a second row of fat molecules lines up tail-to-tail with the outer layer, heads facing inward. With this structure creating an inside and an outside, life can do its work.

principle: a basic truth
maintained: kept up

From: Hoagland, Mahlon, and Bert Dodson. *The Way Life Works: Everything You Need To Know About The Way All Life Grows, Develops, Reproduces, And Gets Along.* Times Books, a division of Random House, Inc.

NOTEZONE

Why do the heads of the fat molecules in the outer row of the cell membrane face outward?

FIND OUT MORE

SCIENCESAURUS

Cells	076
Animal Cell	077
Plant Cell	078

▲ **Cell membrane**

11

Activity

MAKE COMPARISONS The cell membrane controls the movement of nutrients, water, salts, and other substances into the cell and the movement of wastes out of the cell. The membrane also keeps out harmful bacteria, viruses, and other things that could damage the cell.

Water and other materials pass through the membrane and into or out of the cell by a process called *osmosis*. Using an egg to represent a cell, you can see osmosis in action.

WHAT YOU'LL NEED:
- 1 raw egg
- 3 large clear plastic cups
- vinegar
- corn syrup
- water
- 25-cm piece of string
- metric ruler

1. Measure the circumference of the egg by wrapping the string around the egg's middle. Then measure that distance with the ruler. Record that measurement in the chart below.

2. Put the egg in one of the cups, and cover it with vinegar. Leave the cup in the refrigerator for three nights. Examine and measure the egg each day, and record your observations.

3. Carefully take the egg out of the cup. (The shell should be dissolved.) Rinse the egg with water and carefully measure its circumference again.

4. Put the egg in the second cup and cover it with corn syrup. Leave the cup in the refrigerator overnight.

5. Rinse the egg with water, measure its circumference, and put it in the third cup. This time, cover the egg with water. Leave the cup in the refrigerator overnight. Measure the egg's circumference again.

Day	Circumference	Observations of Egg	Observations of Liquid
Start			
After first night in vinegar			
After second night in vinegar			
After third night in vinegar			
After one night in corn syrup			
After one night in water			

▶ *Why did you need to remove the shell from the egg?*

_____

_____

▶ *What did you observe after you left the egg in syrup? Why do you think this happened?*

_____

_____

_____

▶ *Why didn't the syrup pass into the egg?*

_____

_____

▶ *What did you observe after you left the egg in water? Why do you think this happened?*

_____

_____

_____

▶ Take Action

DRAW DIAGRAMS A pack of wolves approaches a herd of musk oxen and tries to attack and kill a calf. Draw a diagram to show how the herd protects its young. Then draw another diagram to show how the cell membrane protects the cell's contents from attacking bacteria.

Structure of a Cell

All Kinds of Parts

If you think a cell is small, imagine how small the structures inside it must be!

A cell is complex. It contains many smaller structures, called *organelles*. Each organelle has a particular job to do to keep the cell working properly. The organelles are found in the cytoplasm that fills the cell. Organelles in an animal cell include lysosomes, the golgi apparatus, ribosomes, the nucleus, the endoplasmic reticulum, and mitochondria. The diagram on page 17 shows what these organelles look like.

▶ **Before You Read**

STAYING ALIVE All living things need nutrients, water, and air. They need a suitable place to live. They grow and change. In addition, all living things sense and respond to changes inside them and in their surroundings, and they reproduce.

▶ *You just read about what living things need to stay alive. What do you think a single cell needs to do in order to stay alive?*

_____

_____

_____

_____

_____

_____

_____

_____

_____

_____

_____

NoteZone

Jot down a question about cells to ask your teacher.

▶ **Read**

The parts of a cell can be compared to things we know well.

The Cell as a City

The cell itself is...comparable to a small city, with functions assigned to tiny workers within its walls....

Inside the cell membrane, the city of the cell is populated by...little workers, called organelles, that perform the services that keep the cell alive. They can be compared to the workers, factories, and transportation and communication systems that are vital to a working community.

For example...the mitochondria burn the carbohydrate fuel that is taken into the cell.... [M]itochondria are rather like power plants burning coal to make the electricity that keeps the city running....

vital: necessary
burn: combine with oxygen to release energy

From: Shroyer, Jo Ann. *Quarks, Critters, and Chaos: What Science Terms Really Mean.* Prentice Hall General Reference.

FIND OUT MORE

SCIENCESAURUS
Animal Cell   077
Plant Cell   078
Cell Processes   079

SCiLINKS.
THE WORLD'S A CLICK AWAY

www.scilinks.org
Keyword: Cell Structure
Code: GSLD01
Keyword: Eukaryotic Cells
Code: GSLD02

◀ **The city of Miami, Florida**

15

The first person to see a cell was Robert Hooke, a British scientist. In 1665 Hooke used a simple microscope to observe dead cork cells. After his discovery, many centuries passed before scientists learned that cells contain organelles such as mitochondria. Each organelle plays a specific role in helping the cell function.

CELL CITY The reading compared mitochondria to a city's power plants. See if you can match each of the other organelles with a city structure that performs a similar function.

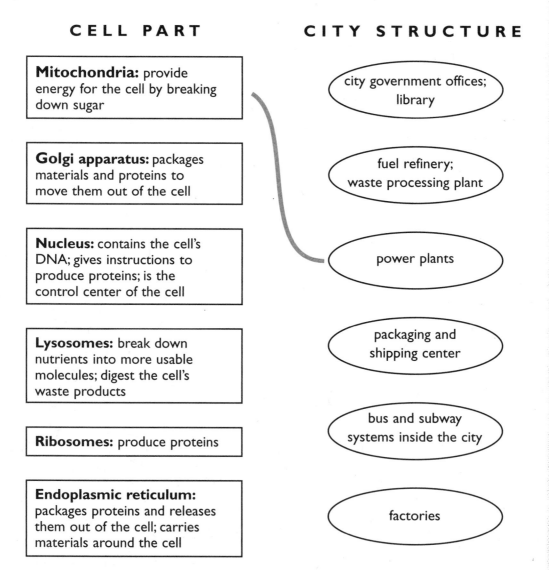

CELL PART

Mitochondria: provide energy for the cell by breaking down sugar

Golgi apparatus: packages materials and proteins to move them out of the cell

Nucleus: contains the cell's DNA; gives instructions to produce proteins; is the control center of the cell

Lysosomes: break down nutrients into more usable molecules; digest the cell's waste products

Ribosomes: produce proteins

Endoplasmic reticulum: packages proteins and releases them out of the cell; carries materials around the cell

CITY STRUCTURE

city government offices; library

fuel refinery; waste processing plant

power plants

packaging and shipping center

bus and subway systems inside the city

factories

WRITE A DIALOGUE A dialogue is a conversation between at least two people. Choose two of the organelles listed on page 16. Then write a dialogue between them in which they argue about which of them is more important to the cell's survival.

_____

_____

_____

_____

_____

_____

_____

_____

_____

_____

_____

_____

ANIMAL CELL

Lysosome

Endoplasmic reticulum

Golgi apparatus

Nucleus

Ribosome

Mitochondrion

Structure of a Cell

The Nucleus and DNA

Every cell contains organelles. But where is the information that tells the organelles what to do? In the nucleus.

All plant and animal cells have a nucleus. The nucleus contains the cell's chromosomes, which are made of DNA. It is the DNA in the nucleus that determines what kind of organism the cell is part of—a frog, an oak tree, a fruit fly, a human, or whatever. Except for egg and sperm cells, the nucleus of every cell in an organism's body has a complete copy of that DNA. Knowing this, scientists searched for a way to produce an entire organism using just a cell's nucleus. In 1997 they finally succeeded.

NOTEZONE

Circle the two things the scientists joined together to create Dolly.

▶ **Read**

Clones: Double Trouble?

Scientists called [Dolly the sheep] "a mind blower," "an awesome work" and "science fiction come true."... Dolly seemed to take her stardom in stride, nibbling straw and blinking softly. But news of her existence caused global excitement.

Dolly is a clone. From the length of her eyelashes to the swirling pattern of her wool, she's an exact copy of another sheep, an adult female, or ewe (pronounced *yew*).

Her life began in a laboratory. Scientists took one cell from a ewe and placed its nucleus, the command center containing the cell's genes, inside a sheep egg cell. The egg's own nucleus had been removed. After a zap of electricity, the cell began behaving like a newly fertilized sheep egg. It divided into more cells. The scientists placed the cluster of cells into the womb of another ewe, where it continued to develop into a lamb. The ewe gave birth to Dolly [in July 1997]. Tests show that she's identical to the ewe whose single cell created her.

From: "Clones: Double Trouble?" *Time for Kids.* Time Inc.
(www.timeforkids.com/TFK/magazines/story/0,6277,93229,00.html)

FIND OUT MORE

SCIENCESAURUS

DNA	115
Genes	116
Cloning	120

Explore

► Why would placing a cell nucleus inside a nucleus-free egg cell enable the egg to begin dividing?

_____

_____

_____

► Why was the new ewe identical to the ewe that the scientists took the cell nucleus from?

_____

_____

_____

Take Action

WRITE A POEM A limerick is a poem with five lines. Lines 1, 2, and 5 rhyme, and each line has 8 to 10 syllables. Lines 3 and 4 rhyme, and each line has 5 or 6 syllables. Write a limerick about Dolly using what you know about the cell nucleus.

_____

_____

_____

_____

_____

_____

_____

_____

_____

Cells at Work

ENERGY FOR LiFE

▼ Structure of a mitochondrion

Inner membrane

Outer membrane

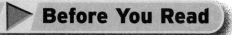

Believe it or not, we humans cannot live without mitochondria!

Mitochondria are one type of organelle found in cell In the mitochondria, the energy that is stored in nutrients is released so the cell can use it.

▶ **Before You Read**

THINK ABOUT IT No organism can survive without energy. How do *you* get and use energy? In the concept map below, list some things in the center box that are sources of energy for your body. In the other boxes, list ways your body uses energy.

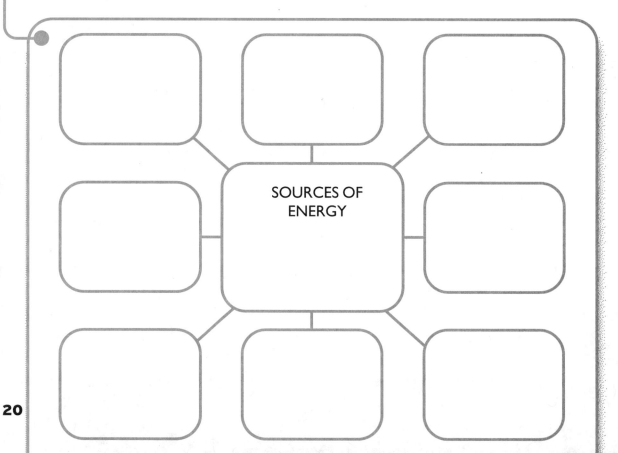

SOURCES OF ENERGY

▶ Read

NOTEZONE

Underline the plural of mitochondrion.

Circle what happens if a mitochondrion can't function.

Draw a box around the name of the fictitious parts of a mitochondrion.

In the science fiction novel *A Wind in the Door*, **Charles Wallace, an unusual six-year-old, has something wrong with his mitochondria. Mr. Jenkins and Margaret, Charles's sister, are trying to find out how to help him.**

Charles Wallace's Mitochondria

"Charles Wallace will die if his mitochondria die. Do you understand that?"

Mr. Jenkins shook his head. "I thought he was making things up with his big words. I thought he was trying to show off. I didn't know there really were mitochondria."

Blajeny turned to Meg. "Explain."

"I'll try. But I'm not sure I really understand either, Mr. Jenkins. But I do know that we need energy to live. Okay?"

"Thus far."

She felt Blajeny kything information to her, and involuntarily her mind sorted it, simplified, put it into words which she hoped Mr. Jenkins would understand. "Well, each of our mitochondria has its own built-in system to limit the rate at which it burns fuel, okay, Mr. Jenkins?"

"Pray continue, Margaret."

"If the number of farandolae in any mitochondrion drops below a critical point, then hydrogen transport can't occur; there isn't enough fuel, and the result is death through energy lack."

Blajeny: a character in the book, a teacher from the universe
kything: in the book, an imaginary way of communicating mind-to-mind, without words

involuntarily: not by choice
farandolae: imaginary microscopic beings that—only in the story—live inside mitochondria

From: L'Engle, Madeline. *A Wind in the Door.* Farrar, Straus, & Giroux.

FIND OUT MORE

SCIENCESAURUS

Animal Cell	077
Cell Processes	079
Animal Physiology	105

▲ **Mitochondrion viewed with a microscope**

EXAMINE AN EQUATION Mitochondria burn fuel to provide our cells with energy. An important chemical reaction called *cellular respiration* takes place in the mitochondria. The chemical equation for cellular respiration looks like this.

$$C_6H_{12}O_6 + 6O_2 \longrightarrow 6CO_2 + 6H_2O + energy$$

glucose + oxygen ⟶ carbon + water + energy
dioxide

WHAT THE EQUATION MEANS During cellular respiration, a type of sugar called glucose is broken down. This happens only with the help of oxygen. Carbon dioxide, water, and energy are given off. Some of the energy is in the form of heat that keeps our bodies warm, and some of the energy is used to keep our cells alive.

FIGURE IT OUT

▶ *Why do we need to breathe in oxygen?*

_____

_____

▶ *Where would you expect to find more mitochondria—in very active cells such as those in your heart and liver, or in less active cells such as those in your earlobes? Explain your answer.*

_____

_____

▶ **Propose Explanations**

DRAW CONCLUSIONS Margaret says that Charles will die if his mitochondria die.

▶ *Knowing what you do about mitochondria, would you agree? Explain your answer.*

_____

_____

_____

_____

_____

► *What would happen to our cells without the mitochondria?*

_____

_____

WRITE A DIALOGUE Imagine that you are Margaret. Any problems your brother had in the past with his mitochondria have been cured. But you're still interested in mitochondria. Write a dialogue, like the one between Margaret and Mr. Jenkins, in which you explain to a friend why mitochondria are important. Include facts that you have learned about what occurs in the mitochondria.

_____

_____

_____

_____

_____

_____

_____

_____

_____

_____

_____

_____

_____

_____

Photosynthesis

You're lucky! You get to eat great-tasting food to get energy. Plants have to make their own food!

Plant cells are different from animal cells. Like animal cells, plant cells have mitochondria, but they also have another kind of energy-converting organelle called a *chloroplast*. Chloroplasts are not found in animal cells.

POWER PLANTS Take a look at a green plant. What are some ways that it obtains the energy and nutrients it needs to stay alive?

_____

_____

_____

 **Read**

A team of Japanese scientists, led by Masamitsu Wada, is studying how chloroplasts move in green plants.

Dancing Chloroplasts

Inside each plant cell, light-gathering chloroplasts dance out of a cell's shaded edges to soak up the sun or back into that shade when the light is too intense....

Chloroplasts...capture light energy from the sun and use it to convert carbon dioxide and water into oxygen and food. The tiny spherical or disk-shaped chloroplasts contain the pigment chlorophyll, which gives green plants their color.

When light is weak, like on a cloudy day, the chloroplasts spread across the upper faces of the cells on a leaf, giving it a deeper green color. In intense sunlight, chloroplasts retreat to the cells' edges, making leaves look pale. Both reactions depend on the amount of...light reaching the cells.

UNIT 1: CELLS

By noting this response in the leaves of [a certain type of plant], Masamitsu Wada...and his [team] identified plants with...copies of a gene...that [lets the plant detect light and tells chloroplasts where to move in the cells].... With this knowledge, the researchers will try to determine [exactly how chloroplasts move]....

intense: strong or concentrated
convert: change
spherical: shaped like a ball
pigment: a colored substance

chlorophyll: a pigment needed for green plants to make food
gene: a section of DNA on a chromosome that determines a particular inherited characteristic

From: Netting, Jessica. "Gene Found For Chloroplast Movement." *Science News.*

NoteZone

Underline the substances plants need to make food.

Draw a box around the other substance that is produced when a plant makes food.

▶ Explore

EXAMINE AN EQUATION A chloroplast has structures that look like stacks of coins. These flat, membrane-covered sacs contain the chlorophyll. Chlorophyll captures the energy in sunlight. The process by which green plants make their own food using the energy in sunlight is called *photosynthesis*. Photosynthesis is a series of chemical reactions that convert light energy into chemical energy contained in glucose. The chemical equation for photosynthesis looks like this.

$$6CO_2 + 6H_2O + \text{light energy} \rightarrow C_6H_{12}O_6 + 6O_2$$

carbon dioxide + water + light energy $\rightarrow$ glucose + oxygen

▲ Chloroplast

WHAT THE EQUATION MEANS During photosynthesis, carbon dioxide gas and water are combined to form glucose. This process requires energy from light. The light energy is changed to chemical energy in glucose. Some of the chemical energy in glucose is released by the plant's mitochondria and used right away, and some of it is stored in other molecules.

MAKE COMPARISONS With their chloroplasts, plants can do something that animals cannot do. What is it?

_____

_____

_____

_____

FIND OUT MORE

SCIENCESAURUS
Plant Cell   078
Cell Processes   079
Plant Physiology   107

SCILINKS.
THE WORLD'S A CLICK AWAY
▼
www.scilinks.org
Keyword: Cell Energy
Code: GSLD03

A LOT O' STOMATA

Plant leaves have tiny openings called *stomata* that take in carbon dioxide and release oxygen. Learn about stomata by doing the following experiment.

FORM A HYPOTHESIS In the experiment, petroleum jelly will clog the stomata on some leaves.

▶ *What do you think will happen to those leaves? Write your hypothesis as an "if / then" sentence.*

_____

_____

What You Need:
- 1 healthy plant
- petroleum jelly

What to Do:
1. Rub a thick layer of petroleum jelly on the top side of three leaves.
2. Apply the jelly to the underside of three other leaves.
3. Leave all the other leaves uncoated as the control.
4. Place the plant in a sunny location for one week.
5. Each day, turn the plant one-quarter turn.
6. Keep the soil moist, but be sure not to overwater the plant.
7. Record your observations each day for one week.

What Do You See?

Day	Leaves with petroleum jelly on top side	Leaves with petroleum jelly on underside	Leaves with no petroleum jelly
1			
2			
3			
4			
5			
6			
7			

DRAW CONCLUSIONS

▶ *Based on your observations, where do you think the stomata are located on leaves? What is your evidence?*

_____
_____
_____
_____
_____
_____

▶ *Go back and look at your hypothesis. Do your results support your hypothesis? How can you tell?*

_____
_____
_____
_____
_____
_____

INVESTIGATING FURTHER Could the rubbing of the leaves have destroyed the stomata? To test this idea, repeat the activity using water instead of petroleum jelly on some leaves. Compare the results of the two activities.

_____
_____
_____
_____
_____
_____
_____

Cells at Work

All Together Now

Now you can put it all together—the mitochondria and the chloroplasts.

Life is filled with many kinds of cycles. Chloroplasts and mitochondria are involved in a cycle that is necessary for the lives of plants and animals. Through the processes of cellular respiration and photosynthesis, plants and animals get materials they need from each other.

NOTEZONE

Underline the two ways glucose is used by plants.

Circle the two gases that are involved in both respiration and photosynthesis.

▶ **Read**

A student wrote to a scientist to find out whether all plants need to respire. This is what the scientist had to say.

From Sugar-Making to Sugar-Burning

Question: Do all plants respire?

Answer: Yes, all plants must carry out respiration. There are two types of respiration processes in plants. One is similar to our breathing process—the plant takes in oxygen through its leaves and releases carbon dioxide. The second type of respiration, called cellular respiration, occurs in the plant cells' mitochondria. This process releases energy that the plant cells need in order to carry out life processes such as growth and reproduction. In the mitochondria, oxygen is combined with glucose, a form of sugar. Carbon dioxide, water, and energy are released.

Energy is also used for photosynthesis. In that process, plants capture the energy in sunlight and use it to convert carbon dioxide and water to glucose. Some of the glucose is transformed into energy through cellular respiration. The rest is used for the plant's life processes. Any "extra" glucose is stored in certain parts of the plant, such as the fruits and vegetables we eat.

Photosynthesis releases much more oxygen than the plant needs for cellular respiration, so the plant releases the "extra" oxygen into the air. We use the oxygen we breathe in our own cellular respiration.

From: *MadSci Network.* Washington University Medical School. (www.madsci.org)

FIND OUT MORE

SCIENCESAURUS
Cell Processes 079

SCILINKS.
THE WORLD'S A CLICK AWAY

www.scilinks.org
Keywords:
Photosynthesis
Code: GSLD04
Cellular Respiration
Code: GSLD05

Explore

REEXAMINE THE EQUATIONS Review the chemical equations for cellular respiration and photosynthesis.

Cellular Respiration

$$C_6H_{12}O_6 + 6O_2 \rightarrow 6CO_2 + 6H_2O + energy$$

glucose + oxygen $\rightarrow$ carbon dioxide + water + energy

Photosynthesis

$$6CO_2 + 6H_2O + light\ energy \rightarrow C_6H_{12}O_6 + 6O_2$$

carbon dioxide + water + light energy $\rightarrow$ glucose + oxygen

MAKE A COMPARISON

▶ *How are the processes of cellular respiration and photosynthesis alike? How are they different?*

_____

_____

_____

_____

_____

_____

_____

▶ *What products does cellular respiration release that are needed for photosynthesis?*

_____

▶ *What products does photosynthesis produce that are needed for cellular respiration?*

_____

SHOW RELATIONSHIPS You are going to explain cellular respiration, photosynthesis, and the relationship between these two processes to another class. Make a poster to use as a visual aid. Include a chloroplast and a mitochondrion on the poster, and use arrows to show the relationship between their two processes. Write a brief paragraph outlining what you will say to the other students.

Cell Division

One Becomes Two

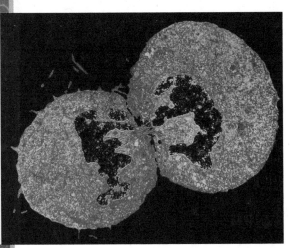

Every living thing begins as a single cell. But many organisms have lots of cells. Where do all the cells come from?

One characteristic of all living things is the ability to reproduce. This includes individual cells. If cells couldn't reproduce to make complete, new cells, life on Earth would cease to exist.

◄**Human kidney cell dividing**

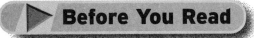

▶ Before You Read

SPLIT IT Lots of things get divided in two. You cut a sandwich in half. You share a banana with your friend. You draw a line down a sheet of paper to make two columns.

▶ *List 10 different things that get divided in two.*

_____

_____

_____

_____

_____

_____

_____

_____

_____

_____

Read

All cells in your body contain identical sets of chromosomes. The chromosomes are made up of DNA (deoxyribonucleic acid) and proteins. The instructions for making all of your different proteins are in the DNA. Various proteins are needed for growth, reproduction, and cell functioning.

Circle the part of the cell that contains the instructions for making proteins.

Where Do Cells Come From?

Whenever fresh cells are needed, a parent cell divides itself into two parts. Two new cells are formed, called daughter cells. What a great idea! Parents turn into children again!

Cell division is not…easy. The new daughter cells must be more or less identical to the parent cell. They need the same genes so that they can create the same proteins. Therefore, equal distribution of the DNA is key to cell division. The DNA wrapped up in the chromosomes must be doubled; each daughter cell can then receive its own copy of chromosomes. Here we can see how that works.

Underline the structures that contain the DNA.

◀ 1. Each human cell has 23 pairs of chromosomes. When a cell gets ready to divide into two, each chromosome doubles.

◀ 2. The nucleus gets ready to divide. The chromosome pairs are connected at the center and form an "X" shape.

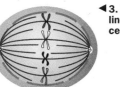

◀ 3. The chromosomes line up across the center of the cell.

▼ 4. The chromosome pairs separate into two individual, identical chromosomes and move to opposite sides of the cell.

▼ 5. The cell splits into two. Each new cell has one full set of chromosomes.

FIND OUT MORE

SCIENCESAURUS

Cell Division	080
Stages of Cell Division	081
DNA	115

SCiLINKS.
THE WORLD'S A CLICK AWAY

www.scilinks.org
Keyword: Mitosis
Code: GSLD06

----

gene: a section of DNA on a chromosome that determines a particular inherited characteristic

proteins: substances that make up living things

distribution: division or "handing out" of something

From: Baeurele, Patrick, and Norbert Landa. *The Cell Works: An Expedition Into the Fantastic World of Cells.* Barron's Education Series, Inc.

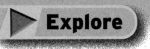

DESIGN A MODEL Create a model to show the five steps in the division of a cell nucleus with six chromosomes. You and your classmates could represent the cell parts, or you could use materials such as yarn and construction paper. Draw and label your model below.

▶ Propose Explanations

EXPLAIN YOUR MODEL

▶ *What did you use to represent the six chromosomes?*

_____

▶ *How did you show the doubled chromosomes?*

_____

_____

▶ *How did you show the movement of the chromosomes?*

_____

_____

_____

▶ *How did you show the two new cells?*

_____

_____

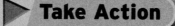
DO RESEARCH The number of chromosomes in a cell is the same in all individuals of a species. All human body cells, except sperm and egg cells, contain 46 chromosomes. But different species of organisms have different numbers of chromosomes. Do research to find out the number of chromosomes in the cells of other species. Start with fruit flies and potato plants. Then add other organisms that you find in your research. Record your findings in the table.

NUMBER OF CHROMOSOMES PER CELL	
Species	Number of Chromosomes
Human	46
Fruit flies	
White potato plants	
Sweet potato plants	

▲ **Fruit fly**

► *Based on your findings, do you think the number of chromosomes gives a clue about how complex an organism is? Explain your answer.*

_____

_____

_____

_____

_____

_____

_____

_____

THE SORCERER'S APPRENTICE

Watch out! Those cells will take over before you know it!

You might think that when an organism grows, its cells increase in size. However, except for one-celled organisms, all organisms grow by producing new cells.

 **Before You Read**

THINK ABOUT IT Suppose someone offered you a choice. You could get one penny the first day, two pennies the second day, four pennies the third day, eight pennies the fourth day, and so on for one month. The amount you get each day would be double the number you received the day before. Or you could get one million dollars. Which would you choose? Why?

_____

_____

_____

_____

_____

_____

_____

_____

_____

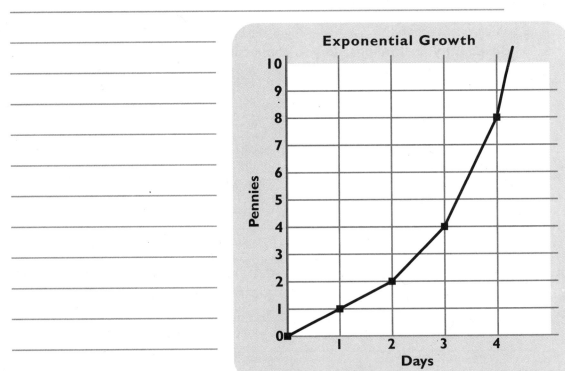

NoteZone

Circle the number of cells present after two divisions.

▶ **Read**

Exponential Growth

All cells grow. They double their size by doubling everything they're made of. Then they exactly double their DNA and divide in half. Two completely new cells replace [the parent cell].

We each began as…a single cell. This cell divided, and then divided again, and then again. Doubling over and over—2 producing 4, producing 8, etc.—quickly leads to large numbers. If all these early cells divided at the same rate, it would take only about 30 divisions to make the many billions of cells of a newborn human….

Cell division is essential…to produce [a complete human being] from an egg. [It is also needed] to replace cells lost during an organism's lifetime by wear and tear and by…cell death.

....

essential: necessary
wear and tear: damage caused by ordinary activities

From: Hoagland, Mahlon, and Bert Dodson. *The Way Life Works: Everything You Need To Know About The Way All Life Grows, Develops, Reproduces, And Gets Along.* Times Books, a division of Random House, Inc.

FIND OUT MORE

SCIENCESAURUS
Kinds of Graphs	390
Line Graphs	394

▼ **Fertilized human egg**

THE GREAT DIVIDE

You can show how fast the number of cells increases when cells divide repeatedly. All you have to do is fold a sheet of paper.

What You Need:
- a thin sheet of paper, preferably tissue paper

What to Do:

1. Begin with a sheet of paper to represent the original parent cell.
2. Fold the sheet of paper in half. Each section represents one daughter cell. Record the number of "cells" in the table.
3. Fold the paper in half again. Record the number of daughter cells.
4. Repeat step 3 as many times as you can.

Fold #	Number of Cells
0	1
1	
2	
3	
4	
5	
6	
7	
8	

What Do You See?

▶ *How many times could you fold the paper? How many sections did you make?*

_____

▶ *Did you see a pattern? If so, what is it?*

_____

_____

MAKE COMPARISONS If you could fold a sheet of paper 14 times, it would be as thick as you are tall. If you could fold it 30 times, its thickness would reach to the edge of the atmosphere, and it would have 1,073,041,824 sections. Fifty folds would create a thickness almost the distance to the sun. One hundred folds? Your paper's thickness would be about the same as the radius of the known universe!

▶ Propose Explanations

COMPARING MODELS A model is a useful tool for showing a complex process in a way that makes it more understandable. Each model has some parts that work the same way as the process it shows. Each model also has some parts that do not work quite the same way as the process.

Compare the paper-folding model you just made with the penny-multiplying model on page 34.

▶ *In each model, how does the number of items (pennies or paper sections) change?*

_____

_____

Compare the two models to the actual process of cell division.

▶ *How is the penny model like cell division? How is it different?*

_____

_____

_____

_____

_____

▶ *How is the paper-folding model like cell division? How is it different?*

_____

_____

_____

_____

_____

▶ *Starting with one parent cell, how many cell divisions are needed to produce more than one thousand daughter cells? Explain how you got your answer.*

_____

_____

_____

_____

Cells Out of Control

Cancer is not a modern disease. It has been around since ancient times.

Doctors want to help people who have cancer live longer. They are working hard to find ways to cure this disease. To do this, they need to know a lot about how cells divide and why.

▶ **Read**

NOTEZONE

Number the ways that cell regulation can go wrong.

There is no signal that causes cancer to start. In fact, cancer starts because a signal that *should* happen *doesn't* happen.

Cell Activity Gone Wrong

Question: What exactly is cancer?

Answer: Think of cancer as uncontrolled cell division. Cell division is very important, such as when the body is growing or healing. Our cells have many controls in place to see that this process happens only when needed. Normal, healthy cells divide only when told to do so. Cancer cells divide without regulation and when they should not.

Why do cancers arise? Well, much work has been and continues to be done by scientists to answer this important question. Most cancer cells have gained mutations, or changes, in their genetic material that affect cell regulation. These mutations may turn off normal controls or leave cell division signals permanently on so the cell thinks it should always divide. Other mutations can affect how quickly the cell divides, and whether it can leave its current place and travel to other parts of the body to form new tumors. Some cancer cells are even able to bring blood from the body to "feed" tumors oxygen and nutrients.

regulation: control

tumors: growths of cells that are not normal

From: *MadSci Network*. Washington University Medical School. (www.madsci.org)

FIND OUT MORE

SCIENCESAURUS

Cell Division	080
Immune System	098

▶ Propose Explanations

MAKE COMPARISONS Cells have a built-in cycle that tells them how to grow, when to divide, when to stop dividing, and when to die. Sometimes a cell changes, or mutates, and its cycle doesn't work as it should. The reasons why this change occurs are not well understood, but it can cause the cell and its daughter cells to divide faster than in the normal cycle. The cells also don't get the signal to stop, and so they divide out of control. This is what happens in cancer.

▶ *How are normal body cells and cancer cells alike?*

_____

_____

▶ *How are normal body cells and cancer cells different?*

_____

_____

_____

▶ Take Action

DO RESEARCH Use reference books, the library, or the Internet to find out more about one type of cancer. On a separate piece of paper, take notes on what we know about this cancer, its symptoms, how it progresses, and ways of treating it. Compare your findings with those of other students to identify differences between different kinds of cancers. On the lines below, write a question about cancer that you would like scientists to investigate.

_____

_____

_____

_____

_____

When Cells Get Together

All Charged Up

How do cells in the body communicate with each other?

All living things are made of cells. Cells join together to form tissues that perform different functions in the body. Muscles are one kind of human body tissue. Bones are another kind of tissue.

Cells that perform one function may not look exactly like cells that perform another function, but all cells have some things in common. One of those things is electricity. While we usually don't think of living things as being "electric," all cells generate electrical charges.

▶ **Before You Read**

Imagine that two people in different towns need to plan and coordinate a trip. How could they do it? They could talk to each other using electrical signals that travel through telephone lines or by E-mail. The trillions of cells in your body are similar. Cells must work together so the body functions normally.

▶ *How do you think the body's cells might use electricity to work together?*

_____

_____

_____

_____

_____

_____

▲ **Human nerve cells**

▶ **Read**

NOTEZONE

Draw a diagram to show how a pain signal travels from your finger to your brain. Label the places where electricity is used.

Jerry wanted to know where in the human body electricity was generated, so he asked Dr. Universe.

THE BODY ELECTRIC

Dear Dr. Universe,

How or where or what organs actually produce the electric[ity] that powers the human body?

Thank you,
Jerry

From: Ask Dr. Universe

Well, you're right about the body being "powered" by electricity. Actually, it uses electricity to communicate with itself. But there is no single organ in the body that produces [all] the electricity. Rather,...every cell in the body produces it. That's right—every single cell!

Some cells generate more [electricity] than others.... The amount depends on what the cells do and what they use the electricity for. Nerve cells and heart cells generate a lot of electricity. Nerve cells use it to transmit messages over long distances.

Suppose, for example, that you burn your finger. A nerve fiber (which is really one cell) uses electricity to send that pain signal all the way from your finger to your spinal cord. There, it makes a chemical signal to another cell, which sends another electrical signal to the brain. And there, somehow the signal gets interpreted as pain....

Other cells that use a lot of electricity are heart cells. They use electricity to control the beating of the heart.

[If you] add up the electricity generated by all the trillions of cells in the body...what you get is enough to light a 40 watt light bulb.

- -

generate: produce
nerve cells: cells that send and receive information

transmit: send
interpreted: made sense of

From: "The BIG Questions." *Ask Dr. Universe*. Washington State University. (www.wsu.edu/DrUniverse/body.html)

FIND OUT MORE

SCIENCESAURUS
Cells   076
Tissues, Organs,
  and Systems   082
Nervous System   095

INTERPRET A SCIENTIFIC DIAGRAM How do cells generate electricity? They can't plug into electrical outlets or use batteries! Instead, they use atoms and molecules with negative and positive charges. These charged atoms and molecules, called ions, are found in some chemicals in the body.

To generate electricity, the cell first pumps out positive ions (+) through tiny spaces in the cell membrane. Now the inside of the cell has more negative ions (−) than positive ions. With more negative ions, the inside of the cell has a negative charge. The outside of the cell has more positive ions than negative ions, so the outside has a positive charge. This diagram shows where those charges are inside and outside the cell.

Objects that have positive and negative electric charges attract one another. If they are separated and given the chance to come back together, positive charges will rush toward negative charges. Electric current is the movement of electric charges.

▶ *What happens to generate electricity?*

_____

_____

_____

▶ *The flow of electricity creates a signal. What kind of signal might a nerve fiber send from a burned finger to the spinal cord?*

_____

A nerve cell's function is to send electrical signals to other parts of the body. A skin cell's function is to act as a barrier between the body and the outside world.

▶ *Where do you think there is more electrical activity—in nerve cells or skin cells? Why?*

_____

_____

Propose Explanations

MAKE INFERENCES Why do cells need to communicate? Think about what happens when you're in pain. You feel pain when nerve cells use electricity to send signals to cells in your spinal cord and then your brain.

► *Imagine you're climbing a tree and you scrape the skin of your hand on the bark. How would your body react?*

_____

_____

► *What purpose do you think pain serves?*

_____

_____

_____

► *What might happen if we didn't feel pain?*

_____

_____

Take Action

RESEARCH REFLEXES A reflex is a reaction the body makes without thinking about it first. The electrical signal travels from the nerve cells of the body part that is in danger to the spinal cord. In a fraction of a second, the spinal cord sends an electrical signal back to the body part "telling" it to move away from the source of danger. A split second later, another electrical signal travels up the spinal cord to the brain. Then the brain interprets the signal as pain. If you've ever been to the doctor for a checkup, you know that one reflex you have is a "knee-jerk" when the front of your knee is tapped. What other reflexes do humans have? Do some research to find out about other reflexes. How does each reflex help humans survive in their environment?

_____

_____

_____

_____

When Cells Get Together

Growing Tissue

How do cells "know" what kind of tissue to form? Scientists are beginning to find out.

Astronauts returning from space often have trouble walking on land. This is because in the "weightlessness" of space, their muscle tissue begins to break down. Scientists worried that astronauts traveling on long space missions might suffer severe tissue damage.

To study the effects of "weightlessness" on human body tissue, scientists at the National Aeronautics and Space Administration (NASA) developed the Bioreactor. This rotating can of liquid nutrients mimics the conditions experienced by astronauts in space. But scientists soon found a new use for the Bioreactor—growing new tissue from cells.

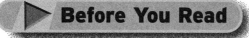
Before You Read

TISSUE ISSUES Tissues are made of identical cells that joined together to perform a specific function.

▲ **Bioreactor**

▶ *Why do you think scientists are interested in growing new tissue?*

_____

_____

_____

_____

_____

_____

_____

_____

▶ **Read**

NOTEZONE

What do you want to know more about after reading this?

The Bioreactor is being used to grow human tissue.

Tissue Engineering

If you've ever seen a pile of ivy that has taken the shape of an old barn...it has overgrown, you've seen the principle that researchers are following in trying to grow replacement parts for bodies....

For many people, culturing cells means putting some small number into...a dish [with liquid nutrients]...and letting them grow. However, this kind of approach does not provide the...environment that supports tissue [formation]. Without a proper 3-D assembly, epithelial [stem] cells...lack the proper clues for growing into the [specific] cells that make up a particular tissue.

The Bioreactor was developed by NASA to simulate the ["weightless"] environment of space by putting cells in a [liquid-filled container] that constantly rotates and keeps the cells in endless free-fall.... In a rotating Bioreactor, the cells can be fooled into thinking they are in a body. With a plastic lattice to help direct their growth, cells can be encouraged to grow [into certain] shapes, just as the...barn gives shape to [the] vines [that cover it].

principle: a rule that determines how a process works

culturing: growing living cells or tiny organisms in a protected environment with nutrients

3-D: three-dimensional; having length, width, and depth

assembly: structure

epithelial stem cells: cells from an adult's skin that can specialize into different kinds of cells

free-fall: a falling motion that is affected only by gravity, not by a parachute or other object

lattice: a structure that something grows over and around

From: "Scientists Grow Heart Tissue In Bioreactor." *Science@NASA*. NASA. (science.nasa.gov/newhome/headlines/msad05oct99_1.htm)

FIND OUT MORE

SCIENCE SAURUS
Cells 076
Tissues, Organs, and Systems 082

SCiLINKS
THE WORLD'S A CLICK AWAY

www.scilinks.org
Keyword: Tissues and Organs
Code: GSLD07

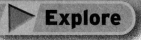

INTERPRET A SCIENTIFIC DIAGRAM The following diagram compares how cells act when they are grown in two different environments— a laboratory dish and the "weightless" environment of the Bioreactor. In both environments, the cells are placed in a liquid that contains nutrients they need in order to survive.

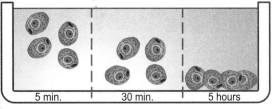

Cells grown in laboratory dish

5 min. 30 min. 5 hours

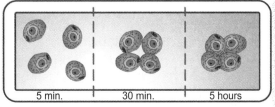

Cells grown in Bioreactor

5 min. 30 min. 5 hours

▶ *After 30 minutes, how have the cells in the laboratory dish moved?*

_____

_____

▶ *What force is causing their movement?* _____

▶ *After 30 minutes, how have the cells in the Bioreactor moved?*

_____

▶ *Compare how the cells in the two containers are arranged after five hours. What do you notice?*

_____

_____

_____

_____

_____

DRAW CONCLUSIONS

▶ *How does the Bioreactor encourage tissue growth more than the laboratory dish does?*

_____

_____

_____

_____

▶ Propose Explanations

MAKE INFERENCES There are many different kinds of cells. Cells that come together to form tissues are specialized to perform that tissue's function. For example, heart muscle cells form heart tissue. The muscles contract and relax to keep blood moving throughout the body.

Stem cells are cells that have not yet become specialized. Stem cells can become any kind of cell. Some stem cells, like the ones used in the experiment, are found in adults. Others are found in developing organisms, such as a fetus in its mother's uterus. When an organism is first forming, it has many stem cells. As the organism begins to form tissues, its stem cells become specialized. Some become skin cells. Others become heart cells. Still others become nerve cells. Scientists don't yet understand exactly how stem cells "know" which kind of specialized cells to become, but they are working on some ideas.

▶ *Based on the reading, what can you infer about where stem cells get the clues to follow in order to become specialized cells?*

_____

_____

▶ *How might scientists use this information to create different types of tissues? (Hint: Recall the example of the barn.)*

_____

_____

▶ Take Action

WRITE A HAIKU A haiku is a form of poetry from Japan. The poem has only three lines, and each line has a set number of syllables: 5, 7, and 5. Unlike some poems, the words in a haiku do not rhyme. The following is an example of a haiku. Count the syllables in each line. Write the number at the end of each line.

Water falls in drops _____

collecting in a smooth pool _____

blue and green and white. _____

Create your own haiku about how cells form tissues or how tissue grows in a Bioreactor. Make sure your haiku has three lines and that each line has the correct number of syllables.

When Cells Get Together

Organ Misfire

What happens when an organ stops functioning normally?

Tissues in the body join together to form organs. Organs perform specific functions, just as cells and tissues do. Organs work together in systems to carry out important life processes.

One system in your body is the endocrine system. The organs in this system are known as *glands*. Glands release substances called *hormones* that act as chemical messengers throughout the body.

One gland in the endocrine system is the thyroid gland. It controls growth and metabolism—the rate at which your body uses energy. People whose thyroid gland isn't working properly can experience many different problems.

Thyroid gland

▶ Before You Read

FIND YOUR THYROID The thyroid is a butterfly-shaped organ located under the skin in the front of your neck. To find it, touch your "Adam's apple" with one finger and the top of your breastbone (just below the little depression at the base of your neck) with your thumb. The thyroid is in that space between your fingers.

▶ Read

Janie hadn't been feeling well. After hearing about her symptoms and having some tests done, Janie's doctor was able to figure out that one of her organs wasn't working properly.

HYPERTHYROID BLUES

Janie didn't notice the changes very much at first—but her teachers did. Since starting sixth grade, Janie had become restless. She was squirmy and nervous, and it was hard for her to sit still in class. Paying attention was hard, too. Finally, Janie's teachers asked the school nurse to call her father.

Janie's dad had noticed some changes as well. She was eating more than usual. But instead of gaining weight, Janie was getting thinner. And even though it was almost December, she was sweating a lot.

FIND OUT MORE

SCIENCESAURUS

Tissues, Organs,
  and Systems   082
Endocrine System 097

He decided it was time for Janie to have a checkup. It didn't take Janie's doctor long to discover what was wrong. Janie had [an overactive] thyroid gland.

Kids with hyperthyroidism can feel jumpy and have trouble concentrating. Like Janie, their hearts might beat fast and their hands may tremble. They can sweat a lot and have trouble sleeping. And even though they might have more of an appetite, they often lose weight or stop gaining it as they grow.

hyperthyroidism: a condition in which the thyroid gland produces too much of its hormone

tremble: shake

From: "Thyroid Disorders." *KidsHealth*. The Nemours Foundation.
(kidshealth.org/kid/health_problems/gland/thyroid.html)

NOTEZONE

Before you read that Janie had an overactive thyroid, what did you think was wrong with her?

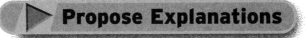 **Propose Explanations**

In the chart below, list the symptoms of hyperthyroidism. Then use a science or health textbook or another reference to decide which organs or organ systems are affected by hyperthyroidism.

Symptom	Organ or Organ System Affected by Condition

▶ *What does this chart tell you about how organs and organ systems in the human body are connected?*

_____

_____

_____

_____

_____

Heredity, Diversity, and Change

How does a species change over time?

You may think that one type of animal will look exactly the same forever. But in fact species change over the course of generations. Why would a species change? If the species' environment changes, the species may change to survive in the new environment.

There's a code inside cells that determines what an organism will become, what it will look like, and why it will be different from another: the genetic code. In this unit, you'll explore how differences in this code can change the size of a cob of corn or the color of a pea plant's flowers. You'll also find out how scientists use genes to help group and identify organisms. And you'll learn that genes determine a lot about you…but not everything.

? Did You Know?

DNA is the material in your cells that determines your inherited characteristics. Almost every bit of your DNA, 99.9 percent, is exactly the same as every other human being's DNA. It's the other 0.1 percent that makes you different from all other people on Earth.

THE CHAPTERS IN THIS UNIT ARE . . .

CHAPTER 5:

How Genes Work

Find out: How did Native Americans create corn with longer cobs?

CHAPTER 6:

Genes and People

Find out: Why do certain people in Kentucky have blue-tinged skin?

CHAPTER 7:

Most Likely to Survive

Find out: Why is the gene to grow tusks disappearing from some elephant populations?

CHAPTER 8:

One Hundred Million Kinds of Things

Find out: What happens when scientists discover a brand-new organism?

How Genes Work

Your Genes and Chromosomes

What makes you "you" and different from your friends or even the other members of your family? Three letters say a lot: DNA.

Who you are depends on lots of things, including how you are brought up and the choices you make. But each of us has a "book of life" in our cells that tells most of the story about who we are and how we grow. That "book," the book of *your* life, is given to you by your biological parents. It helps determine how your body looks, functions, and responds to the things around you. Your "book of life"—your genome—is coded in something called deoxyribonucleic acid, or DNA.

NOTEZONE

What else would you like to know about your genome?

▶ **Read**

Here is how science writer Matt Ridley describes the genome.

The Book of Life

Imagine that the genome is a book. There are twenty-three chapters, called chromosomes. Each chapter contains several thousand stories called genes.

There are one billion words in the book, which makes it longer than 5,000 volumes. If I read the book out loud to you for eight hours a day, it would take me a century. This is a gigantic document, an immense book and it all fits inside the microscopic nucleus of a tiny cell that fits easily upon the head of a pin.

Instead of being written on flat pages, genomes are written on long chains called DNA molecules. Each chromosome is one pair of (very) long DNA molecules.

genome: all the genes of an organism

chromosomes: strands of DNA in a cell's nucleus that carry the code for the organism's inherited characteristics

gene: a section of DNA on a chromosome that determines a particular inherited characteristic

DNA: the material in a cell's nucleus that determines the organism's genetic traits

molecules: groups of atoms linked together

FIND OUT MORE

SCIENCESAURUS

DNA   115
Genes   116
The Human Genome   117
Heredity   121

SCI LINKS.
THE WORLD'S A CLICK AWAY

www.scilinks.org
Keyword: DNA
Code: GSLD09

From: Ridley, Matt. *Genome: The Autobiography of a Species in 23 Chapters.*
HarperCollins Publishers, Inc.

UNIT 2: HEREDITY, DIVERSITY, AND CHANGE

© GREAT SOURCE. COPYING IS PROHIBITED.

▶ Explore

MAKE COMPARISONS DNA is a very long molecule that carries the information needed to produce an organism and keep it functioning. All the information makes up the organism's genome. The information is organized into genes, which code for (give instructions for) individual physical characteristics, or traits. Genes are gathered together on chromosomes. Science writer Matt Ridley compared this information to a book.

▶ *In what ways is the human genome like a book? In what ways is it different?*

_____

_____

_____

_____

▶ *If your genome were compared to a cookbook, what "recipes" would it include?*

_____

_____

_____

▶ Take Action

USE ANALOGIES Matt Ridley used a book as an analogy for the human genome. An analogy uses an everyday, familiar example to help explain a more complex and less familiar topic. One example of an analogy is *The circulatory system is like a network of major highways, main roads, and small streets.* Create your own analogy to explain a complex science process or structure. Write your analogy below.

_____

_____

_____

_____

_____

How Genes Work

IN-GENE-IUS!

How can garden peas help explain why a father and daughter both have red hair and freckles?

Gregor Mendel was a monk who lived in Austria in the mid-1800s. Mendel spent most of his time in the monastery garden, tending to the pea plants he grew there. He was interested in different physical traits of the plants. For example, he studied how tall they were, what their seeds looked like, and what color flowers they produced. In particular, Mendel was interested in how these traits were inherited, or passed from one generation of plants to the next. Did all pea plants look exactly like their parents? To find out, Mendel conducted experiments over many years.

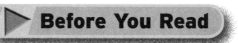 **Before You Read**

MAKE COMPARISONS Examine two or more plants that are the same species. Are the plants identical in every way? Look for differences in color, shape, and size of leaves or flowers, and so on. What do you notice?

▶ *Sketch the plants in the box below. Label any differences you found.*

R46

> **Read**

Scientific breakthroughs require a lot of hard work. Mendel spent many long hours working in his "garden laboratory."

In the Garden

In a corner of the monastery garden, Mendel huddled...over rows of greening [pea] plants. These were functional little vegetable plants, but they held a strange beauty. Climbing along sticks and strings, they twirled and twisted gracefully as they arched toward the...sunshine....

As he moved from one row of pea plants to another, Mendel carefully lifted the leaves away from the slim stalks, pulling at the flowers hidden beneath like coy little butterflies. The leaves were smooth ovals, [reminding him] of cupped hands enclosing something precious; as they gradually unfurled, they revealed a flower, either white or a variation of purple, shaped like a tiny bonnet. These flowers, like those of most plants, were the plant's ovaries. Over time the petals faded and the calyx toughened and elongated, becoming the long, leathery pea pods we recognize easily. Within each pod were six or seven peas, the offspring of the plants on which they grew....

▲ **Pea plant flower**

(labels: Stigma, Petals, Stamens, Pistil, Ovary, Anther, Calyx, Sepals)

monastery: the building where a community of monks live

coy: shy

unfurled: opened up

ovaries: the female reproductive parts of plants that produce seeds

calyx: the outermost ring of petals on a flower

offspring: the young of an organism

From: Henig, Robin Marantz. *The Monk in the Garden.* Houghton Mifflin.

NOTEZONE

Study the diagram of a pea plant flower. On the diagram, (circle) the names of the flower parts that are mentioned in the reading. Where do the peas form?

> **FIND OUT MORE**

SCIENCESAURUS

Sexual Reproduction	114
Genes	116
Heredity	121
Dominant and Recessive Alleles	122

SCiLINKS
THE WORLD'S A CLICK AWAY

www.scilinks.org
Keyword: Mendelian Genetics
Code: GSLD08

© GREAT SOURCE. COPYING IS PROHIBITED.

55

ANALYZE DATA Mendel crossed pairs of pea plants to see what their offspring would look like. One cross he did was between pea plants with purple flowers. Here are the results Mendel got when he crossed purple-flowered plants with each other.

MENDEL'S DATA: CROSSING PURPLE-FLOWERED PLANTS	
Flower Color of Offspring Plants	**Number of Plants**
Purple	705
White	224

▶ *What is the ratio of purple to white flowers in the offspring plants? (In other words, about how many purple-flowered plants are there for every white-flowered plant?)*

▶ *Does anything about these results seem odd to you? If so, explain.*

Mendel hypothesized that pea plants must receive one instruction for flower color from one parent and another instruction for flower color from the other parent. We now know that these instructions are genes. Each parent pea plant contains two genes for the trait of flower color. Each parent gives one gene for flower color to each of its offspring, so each offspring also has two genes for that trait.

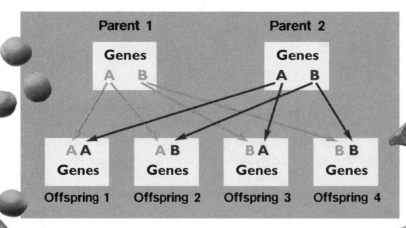

56

▶ Propose Explanations

BLOOMING GENES Mendel noticed that even when a pea plant had parents with two different flower colors, only one color was seen in the offspring plant. Mendel concluded that the other gene must be in the parent plant but not be shown. The trait controlled by the hidden gene he called the *recessive trait*. The trait shown by the plant he called the *dominant trait*. Mendel reasoned that recessive traits weren't seen as often as dominant traits because a plant must have two genes for the recessive trait in order for the trait to show.

▶ *Which flower color do you think is dominant in pea plants? Support your answer with evidence from the chart of Mendel's data.*

_____

_____

▶ *How do you think plants with white flowers could have come from two parent plants with purple flowers?*

_____

_____

▶ Take Action

USING FIGURES OF SPEECH Similes and metaphors are figures of speech used to explain how something acts or looks by comparing it to how something else unrelated to it acts or looks. A simile uses the word "like" or "as" to compare two things—for example, "a flower shaped like a tiny bonnet." A metaphor compares two things without using "like" or "as"—for example, "leathery pea pods."

▶ *Circle the similes and metaphors in the reading. Then create your own similes or metaphors to describe a simple action you perform every day, such as brushing your teeth or taking out the trash. See how using similes and metaphors can make a description of an ordinary task more interesting.*

_____

_____

_____

_____

How Genes Work

CUSTOM CORN

Can a working knowledge of genes help us create a "super vegetable"? It already has.

A tiny potato would be hard to make into a pile of French fries. But what if you crossed two parent plants that produce big potatoes, and then took the offspring with the biggest potatoes and crossed them with other plants that produce big potatoes, and so on for several generations? What kind of potato plant would you get?

THINK ABOUT SEEDS Most plants produce seeds that grow to become new plants. In nature, this happens when the seeds fall from the parent plant and take root in the soil. Gardeners often collect seeds from one year's harvest and plant them the following spring to produce new plants.

► *If you wanted to get seeds from a certain kind of garden plant, which parts of the mature plant would you collect? Describe where you think the seeds are found in the following fruit and vegetable plants.*

Fruit or Vegetable Plant	Location of Seeds
Tomato plant	
Corn stalk	
Cucumber vine	
Pea plant	
Apple tree	

▶ Read

When you butter up that big ear of summer corn, you can thank ancient Native Americans.

How People Changed Corn

Did you know that the first cobs of corn weren't that long...? In fact, scientists have found five-thousand-year-old corncobs that are less than one inch long!

What changed corn? People did.

Native Americans first began growing corn about seven thousand years ago in what is now New Mexico. Soon they noticed many differences between different cobs of corn....

The Native Americans made great use of the differences they observed. In particular, they made use of the differences in length. They found that when they used only longer cobs as parents, the offspring corn tended to be longer. If they were careful to use only the longest cobs as parents generation after generation, the corn got longer and longer. They were changing the species of corn itself!

Now, centuries later, the average cob of corn is ten times longer than its ancient ancestor. Thanks to centuries of this process, you can butter and salt a long cob of corn!

generation: one set of offspring
century: 100 years
ancient: very old
ancestor: a related organism in the past

From: Aronson, Billy. *They Came From DNA*. Henry Holt and Company.

FIND OUT MORE

SCIENCESAURUS
Genes	116
Heredity	121
Dominant and Recessive Alleles	122

59

THINK ABOUT IT Members of a species share most of their physical traits—but not all of them. There is natural variety among individuals. For example, all humans share a basic body plan, but individuals have different hair and skin colors, heights, facial features, and other physical traits. These differences make each of us unique.

▶ *What variation between corn plants did the Native Americans find?*

_____

▶ *How did the Native Americans use this variation to change the corn?*

_____

_____

_____

▶ *Think back to the discoveries Mendel made in his garden. How did the Native Americans use the natural laws of inheritance that Mendel later discovered in his experiments?*

_____

_____

_____

_____

_____

_____

▶ Propose Explanations

GENERATE IDEAS

▶ *Could even longer cobs be produced? How would you do it?*

_____

_____

_____

_____

_____

_____

▶ *Do you think it would be possible to produce plants with cobs that were 1 meter long and had a mass of 20 kilograms? Why or why not?*

_____

_____

_____

_____

CONSIDER THE BENEFITS

▶ *Why do you think Native Americans put time and effort into developing corn plants that produced longer cobs? What advantage would longer cobs give the Native Americans?*

_____

_____

DO RESEARCH Vegetables are not the only living things that can be changed by people. All the dogs we see today are actually members of the same species. Different breeds were produced by crossing parents with desirable traits.

▶ *What is your favorite dog breed? Do some research to find out what traits your favorite breed was bred to have. Why were these traits desirable to the breeder? What task was the dog bred to do? How long has this dog been recognized as a breed?*

_____

_____

_____

_____

_____

_____

_____

Genes and People

Single-Gene Human Traits

Are your earlobes loose from the side of your head? If they are, then your earlobes show a dominant trait.

Most human traits are determined by a combination of several genes. This makes trying to figure out which gene controls which trait very complicated! But a few human traits are determined by a single gene.

GENE COMBINATIONS Since everybody has two biological parents, everybody has two sets of genes—one set from the mother and another set from the father. Each gene in one set pairs up with one gene in the other set. Both genes in each pair control the same trait. But the two genes in the pair might be different forms. For example, one gene in the pair might code for detached earlobes, and the other gene might code for attached earlobes. Or both genes might code for detached earlobes, or both for attached earlobes.

▶ *Can a person have more than two genes for a single trait? Explain.*

_____

_____

One form of the two genes in a pair might override the other form of the gene. The form that shows up in the person is called the *dominant* form of the gene. The form that shows up only when a dominant form is not present is called the *recessive* form. Detached earlobes are produced by the dominant form of the gene. Attached earlobes are produced by the recessive form of the gene.

▶ *What are the possible combinations of dominant and recessive forms of a gene?*

_____

▶ *Which of these combinations would show the dominant trait? Which would show the recessive trait?*

_____

_____

UNIT 2: HEREDITY, DIVERSITY, AND CHANGE

Activity

STATE YOUR TRAIT The chart below lists human traits that are determined by a single gene. Do you show the dominant or recessive form of each trait? Fill in the boxes to show which form you have. In the last column, write the gene combination you might have for each trait.

Trait	Description	Dominant or Recessive	Do I have this trait?	Possible Gene Combination
Detached earlobes	Earlobes hang free from the side of the jaw.	dominant		
Curved little finger	When hand is flat on table, the little finger curves toward other fingers.	dominant		
Thumb on top	When hands are clasped with fingers interlaced, the left thumb is on top.	dominant		
Bent thumb	The end segment of the thumb can be bent back more than 60 degrees.	recessive		
Dimpled chin	The middle of the chin has a dimple or cleft.	dominant		

Take Action

MATCHING TRAITS A girl named Jeanie Trate has a straight little finger, detached earlobes, and a dimpled chin. The chart below lists the gene forms that each possible parent has. Select which mother and father are Jeanie's parents. Explain your answer.

Mother A		Mother B		Father A		Father B	
Curved little finger	Curved little finger	Curved little finger	Straight little finger	Straight little finger	Straight little finger	Curved little finger	Straight little finger
Detached earlobes	Attached earlobes	Attached earlobes	Attached earlobes	Detached earlobes	Attached earlobes	Attached earlobes	Attached earlobes
Dimpled chin	Dimpled chin	Dimpled chin	Undimpled chin	Undimpled chin	Undimpled chin	Dimpled chin	Dimpled chin

_____

_____

_____

_____

FIND OUT MORE

SCIENCESAURUS

Genes 116
Heredity 121
Dominant and
Recessive Alleles 122

Genes and People

The Blue People of Kentucky

Some people inherit blue eyes from their parents. But a group of people in Kentucky inherit blue skin.

A recessive trait can lie hidden in a family's genes for generations before it shows up again. That's because each offspring has to receive the recessive gene from both parents, not just one. Blue-tinged skin is one such recessive trait. It is found among a group of people living in eastern Kentucky. Because the group is relatively small, recessive forms of genes are often paired, and the trait shows up frequently.

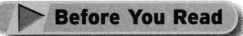 **Before You Read**

WHO AM I? Take a look at your classmates. Does anyone look just like you? No—unless your identical twin is in your class! Does anyone share something in common with you? Well, yes—most have the same basic body features. But does everyone have hair just like yours? What about the shape of your eyes?

▶ *Why do you think people often look like other members of their family?*

_____

_____

_____

UNIT 2: HEREDITY, DIVERSITY, AND CHANGE

Read

Traits make their way through generations as they are passed from parents to offspring.

THE BLUE PEOPLE

Six generations after a French orphan named Martin Fugate settled on the banks of eastern Kentucky's Troublesome Creek with his redheaded American bride, his great-great-great great grandson [Ben Stacy] was born in a modern hospital not far from where the creek still runs.

The boy inherited his father's lankiness and his mother's slightly nasal way of speaking. What he got from Martin Fugate was dark blue skin. "It was almost purple," his father recalls.

Ben lost his blue tint within a few weeks, and now he is about as normal looking a seven-year-old boy as you could hope to find. His lips and fingernails still turn a shade of purple-blue when he gets cold or angry.

After ruling out heart and lung diseases, the doctor suspected methemoglobinemia, a rare hereditary blood disorder…. [The doctor] also concluded that the condition was inherited as a simple recessive trait. In other words, to get the disorder, a person would have to inherit two genes for it, one from each parent. Somebody with only one gene would not have the condition but could pass the gene to a child.

▲ **Martin and Elizabeth Fugate**

lankiness: being tall and thin
nasal: related to the nose

From: Trost, Cathy. "The Blue People of Troublesome Creek." *Science 82*.

NOTEZONE

How could Benjy Stacy have blue skin?

FIND OUT MORE

SCIENCESAURUS

Genes	116
Heredity	121
Dominant and Recessive Alleles	122

SCLINKS
THE WORLD'S A CLICK AWAY

www.scilinks.org
Keyword: Genes and Traits
Code: GSLD10

▶ **Explore**

INTERPRET A DIAGRAM A recessive trait shows up only when someone has two recessive forms of the gene. A person who has only one recessive form of the gene is a carrier of the recessive trait but does not show that trait.

The following diagram shows how the recessive trait that results in blue skin tone is passed down through generations in Troublesome Creek, Kentucky. The dominant gene is for white (non-blue) skin.

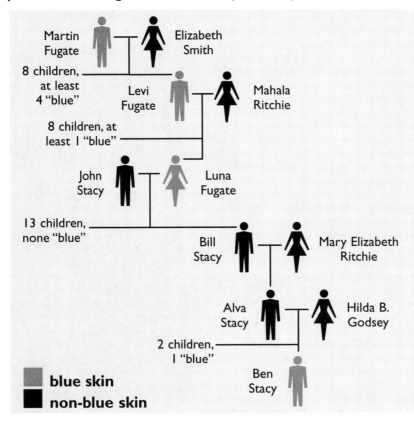

Use the diagram to answer the following questions.

▶ *Can men carry the gene form for blue skin tone? Explain.*

_____

_____

_____

▶ *Can women carry the gene form for blue skin tone? Explain.*

_____

_____

_____

▶ Propose Explanations

THINK ABOUT IT

▶ *Why didn't Bill Stacy have blue skin even though his mother did?*

_____

_____

_____

_____

_____

▶ *How could Ben Stacy have had blue skin when neither of his parents did?*

_____

_____

▶ *Most people in the small Troublesome Creek community are carriers of the recessive blue-skin trait. They also tend to marry within their own community. How do these facts explain why blue-skinned children keep appearing in the population?*

_____

_____

_____

▶ Take Action

WRITE A DIALOGUE Imagine that a husband and wife have just returned from being tested by a doctor, who discovered that they are both carriers of the recessive gene form for sickle-cell anemia. Sickle-cell anemia is a disease of the red blood cells. Instead of being round like normal blood cells, sickle cells are shaped like half-moons. These cells can get stuck in small blood vessels and cause dangerous swellings.

Although neither of the parents has sickle-cell anemia, the doctor explains that there's a one-in-four chance that any child of theirs would have the disease. The husband doesn't understand how his child could possibly inherit a life-threatening disease from him when he doesn't have the disease himself.

▶ *On a separate piece of paper, write a dialogue between the husband and wife in which the wife explains to her husband how recessive genes can be passed down by parents who are carriers.*

Genes and People

MORE THAN JUST GENES

Is there more to us than long strings of DNA molecules? You bet!

Genes are made of DNA, and DNA provides the "recipe" for every cell in your body. So we are simply what our genes make us, right? Think again! Human beings are more than just what is spelled out by DNA. Many of our characteristics are not controlled by genes.

▶ **Before You Read**

WHO ARE YOU? There are a lot of different ways to describe yourself. Some of these ways have to do with your personality and your likes and dislikes. Other ways have to do with what you look like and how your body functions.

▶ *Write down ten words that describe you.*

_____   _____

_____   _____

_____   _____

_____   _____

_____   _____

▼ **Model of a DNA molecule**

UNIT 2: HEREDITY, DIVERSITY, AND CHANGE

▶ Read

NOTEZONE

Circle the things in our environment that influence who we are.

Genes direct part of the story of your life—but not the whole story.

Who We Are

"Creativity runs in the family." "I inherited this bad back." "All the women in my family live past 80." People often wonder how they acquire their traits, from talents to ailments. Genes we inherit from our parents do indeed guide how the body develops and functions. But where we live, what we do—our individual environment, starting in the womb—also plays a large role in determining the outcome.

Nutrition, exercise and education are some of the influences on our health and behavior. Identical twins, for example, share the same genes. But twins develop unique personalities, disabilities, skills, and sometimes looks based on environmental factors.

Researchers are now finding connections between genes and human characteristics ranging from athletic ability to aging. But for the most part, our genes are not our ultimate fate. Instead, we are a product of interactions between genes and our environment....

....

ailments: mild illnesses   **ultimate:** final
womb: uterus; the female
organ in which a baby
develops

From: "Our Genetic Identity." *The Genomic Revolution*. American Museum of Natural History. (www.amnh.org/exhibitions/genomics/1_identity/nature.html)

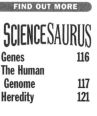

FIND OUT MORE

SCIENCE SAURUS

Genes	116
The Human Genome	117
Heredity	121

WHO'S IN CONTROL? In the previous lesson, you learned about some physical traits that are controlled by genes. What other physical traits do you think are controlled by your genes?

_____

_____

You also learned that there is usually more than one gene involved in determining a physical trait. More than just genes are involved, too.

Look at the following table. The traits in the left column are controlled by your genes. The traits in the right column are controlled by more than just your genes.

Traits Controlled by Genes	Traits Controlled by More Than Genes
Hair color	Athletic ability
Eye color	Personality
Thickness of beard	Tendency to get sick
Shape of fingernails	Response to frustration

▶ *What similarities are there among the traits in the left column? The traits in the right column?*

_____

_____

_____

▶ *How might the traits in the right column be influenced by genes? How might they be influenced by a person's environment?*

_____

_____

_____

_____

▶ Propose Explanations

THINK ABOUT IT Take another look at the traits you listed on page 68. Which traits do you think are determined by your genes? Write *Yes* next to those. Which do you think are not determined by your genes? Write *No* next to those.

▶ *Were some traits difficult to put into one category or the other? Why?*

_____

_____

_____

▶ *Look at the traits you wrote* **No** *next to. What might affect these traits?*

_____

_____

_____

_____

▶ Take Action

TALENT INTERVIEW Do you have a friend who is very good at something? Maybe it's sports or playing a musical instrument. Maybe it's drawing or singing or telling stories. Interview your friend and try to find out whether other people in your friend's family also have that ability. Create a diagram of your friend's family that shows which relatives share that particular ability. Did any family members ever use their ability in this area professionally? What sort of training did they have to develop their ability? Do they think that talent or hard work was more important to their success? Or were they equally important?

▶ *Based on what you learned from the interview, do you think that talent might be determined by the family members' genes? What other factors might have influenced the development of the talent?*

_____

_____

_____

_____

Most Likely to Survive

The Right Stuff

Plants and animals that are well-adapted to their environment are most likely to survive.

◀ **Ruby-throated hummingbird**

For animals, survival means finding food, escaping predators, and adjusting to environmental changes. Plants also face survival challenges, such as getting enough water, nutrients, and sunlight. Some organisms are better equipped for survival in their environment than others. The characteristics that improve an organism's chances of survival are called *adaptations*. Adaptations are passed down from one generation to the next in genes.

▶ **Before You Read**

IDENTIFY STRUCTURES

▶ *Name one of your favorite kinds of wild animals and describe its habitat (the area in which it lives).*

_____

_____

_____

▶ *Identify three body structures that enable the animal to survive in its environment. Briefly describe the function of each structure and how you think it helps the animal survive.*

_____

_____

_____

_____

_____

_____

_____

UNIT 2: HEREDITY, DIVERSITY, AND CHANGE

▶ **Read**

NoteZone

Underline the sentences that describe how a long neck helps giraffes survive.

How did giraffes get their long necks?

Successful Variations

Giraffes have the longest necks of any mammal, which is why they're so tall.... At one time, people imagined that giraffes [evolved] their long necks as they stretched to eat higher leaves. We now know that changes in animals and plants over generations don't occur that way. [Today's] idea, developed by scientists such as Charles Darwin, is that evolution [begins with] variation.

Variation means that sometimes, by accident, an animal will be born that is somehow different from the others of its species. Maybe its legs are built a little differently and it can run faster. Or maybe it's [extremely] slow. Variations aren't necessarily good or bad. They just happen in nature.

...The better [adapted] an animal is to the area it lives in, the better its chances of living a long life and having [offspring]. And the [offspring] may inherit whatever variation made the animal so successful in its environment.

Something like this probably happened with the shorter-necked ancestors of modern giraffes. Those that by chance were born with somewhat longer necks could [reach] farther up into the trees and find more food—a definite survival advantage. So over generations, longer-necked giraffes gradually crowded out shorter-necked ones.

From: Wollard, Kathy. "The Long and Short of Giraffes." *Newsday*.

FIND OUT MORE

SCIENCESAURUS
Heredity   121

73

COMPARE ADAPTATIONS Two animal species that are well-adapted to their environment are the duck-billed platypus and the giraffe. Read the photo captions to learn about each animal's habitat, diet, predators, and adaptations.

PLATYPUS
Habitat: Australia's rivers, lakes, and streams; when not swimming, they live in burrows along the banks of these bodies of water
Diet: includes worms, small shellfish, frog and fish eggs, and other animals from the bottom of streams
Predators: include hawks, eagles, crocodiles, and water-rats
Adaptations: broad tail similar to a beaver's; thick, brown fur; claws on its feet; webs on its front feet that can extend beyond the claws; a duck-like bill

GIRAFFE
Habitat: open grasslands south of the Sahara desert in Central Africa
Diet: tree leaves
Predators: lions; young giraffes are also hunted by leopards, cheetahs, hyenas, and crocodiles
Adaptations: long neck; long, strong legs; patchlike markings on its body; large heart; long tongue; long eyelashes

► *Compare the adaptations that the platypus and giraffe use to move around in their habitats. How do these adaptations help them survive?*

_____

_____

_____

_____

► *What adaptations do the platypus and the giraffe have that help them get food?*

_____

_____

_____

► *What adaptation do you think would help an adult giraffe defend itself if lions attacked? What adaptation would help a platypus avoid a hawk?*

_____

_____

_____

Propose Explanations

CONSIDER CHANGES Adaptations that are useful in one environment may not be useful in another. For example, birds with long, slender beaks have a survival advantage over birds with shorter beaks in an area where nectar is plentiful. But suppose that a disease killed off all the plants in the area that produced flowers with nectar.

► *How would this change affect the bird populations in the area?*

_____

_____

_____

Take Action

INVENT A SPECIES Choose one location you know really well, such as your gym locker, a local movie theater, a computer store, a shopping mall, or a skateboard park. On a separate piece of paper, describe the place you chose. Be as detailed as you can. Then create an imaginary animal with adaptations that would enable it to survive in that environment. How does the animal find food? How does it protect itself from predators? How does it stay warm (or cool)? How does it move around? Which of its senses is the strongest? In the space below, draw a picture of your animal. Label its structures to explain how each one enables the animal to survive in its environment.

Most Likely to Survive

Tall, Gray, and Tuskless

Due to illegal hunting, some Asian elephant populations may be losing the gene for tusks.

When we think of an elephant, we think of a big, gray animal with large ears and long, curved, white tusks. These physical traits are determined by the elephant's genes.

An animal inherits its genes from its parents. Its genes determine which traits the animal has. Its traits can either help the animal survive in its environment or make it difficult or even impossible for the animal to survive. Animals with "helpful" traits have a much better chance of surviving long enough to produce offspring and pass on their genes. Animals with "unhelpful" traits often don't survive long enough to reproduce. Over time, the "unhelpful" traits disappear from the population. Only the "helpful" traits are still passed from one generation to the next. This process is called *natural selection.* Scientists think they are seeing a kind of natural selection in action in certain Asian elephant populations in Sri Lanka.

▲ Asian
elephant

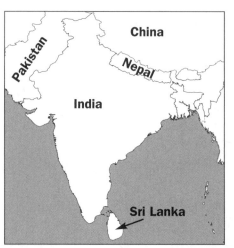

UNIT 2: HEREDITY, DIVERSITY, AND CHANGE

▶ Read

NOTEZONE

If you could interview conservationist Paul Toyne, what's one question you would ask him?

Hunters that kill elephants for their tusks may be unintentionally removing the "tusk gene" from some Asian elephant populations.

More Tuskless Elephants Than Ever

In a woeful version of natural selection, ivory poaching may be causing Asian elephants to lose the gene that allows them to develop tusks....

In contrast to the African species, not all male Asian elephants grow tusks. "The ones that do are the ones being hunted by ivory poachers, so the tusk gene may well disappear from the population," [say] leading international conservationists.

About 40 to 50 percent of [Asian elephants] are normally tuskless, but [on the island of] Sri Lanka, more than 90 percent of the population is not growing tusks.

"When you have ivory poaching, the gene that selects for whether an elephant has tusks or not will be removed from the population," said Paul Toyne, a species conservation officer of the World Wildlife Federation. "Animals that don't have tusks must have some sort of recessive gene, which might normally be shown in the next generation. But once the males with tusks are removed, they will not have the opportunity to pass on these genes. It is an alarming situation."

▲ **Tusks from elephants killed by poachers**

FIND OUT MORE

SCIENCESAURUS

DNA	115
Genes	116
Heredity	121
Dominant and Recessive Alleles	122
The Theory of Evolution	126
Natural Selection	127

SCILINKS
THE WORLD'S A CLICK AWAY

www.scilinks.org
Keyword: Natural Selection
Code: GSLD11

---

woeful: full of sadness

ivory poaching: the illegal killing of elephants to obtain their tusks, which are made of ivory

gene: segment of DNA that determines the inheritance of a particular trait

conservationist: a person who protects endangered species and their habitats

recessive gene: one of a pair of genes that is masked if a dominant gene is present

From: "Poaching Creates Tuskless Elephants," *United Press International.*

ELEPHANT WALK

In this simplified model, you'll see how some Asian elephant populations are changing as a result of ivory poaching. In this model, white jellybeans will represent adult elephants with tusks. Red jellybeans will represent adult elephants that never developed tusks.

The natural selection of genetic traits sometimes happens over a long period of time, even millions of years. But other times, a species' genes are altered in only a few years. What is causing the tusk gene to disappear from Asian elephant populations? To understand the answer, consider two important factors.

- The poachers usually kill only elephants that have tusks. Tuskless elephants aren't killed because they are not a source of ivory.
- Adult male elephants that don't have tusks do not have the gene for growing tusks.

What You Need:
- 20 white jellybeans
- 30 red jellybeans
- small paper bag

What to Do:
1. Select a partner. Decide which one of you will represent a forest where Asian elephants live and which one will represent an ivory poacher. (You'll change places each round.)
2. Put 20 white and 20 red jellybeans into the paper bag and mix them up. Give the bag to the "forest."
3. The "ivory poacher" reaches into the bag without looking and removes one jellybean.
   - If the jellybean is white (tusks), the "poacher" eats it. This represents a poacher killing the elephant.
   - If the jellybean is red (no tusks), the "poacher" puts it back in the bag and adds two more red jellybeans to represent the tuskless elephant's offspring.
4. Repeat step 3 four more times, switching roles with your partner each time.

What Do You See?

With your partner, count the white jellybeans (elephants with tusks) and the red jellybeans (elephants without tusks). Record your results in the following chart. Compare these results with the number of white and red jellybeans you started with.

	RED JELLYBEANS	WHITE JELLYBEANS
Start	20	20
End		

WHAT DO YOU THINK?

▶ *Explain what happened to the numbers of white and red jellybeans after you repeated step 3 five times.*

_____

_____

_____

▶ *How does this model show what is happening to some Asian elephant populations in Sri Lanka?*

_____

_____

_____

_____

_____

_____

▶ Take Action

WHY IVORY? Even though the international ivory trade was outlawed in 1989, elephants continue to be hunted for their tusks. Research some of the products that ivory has been used for over the years. Then find out what alternative materials are used instead of ivory.

Most Likely to Survive

New and Improved

Fruit bat ◄

Through the process of natural selection, an amazing number of different species of organisms have evolved on Earth.

Don't be fooled by appearances. Just because two different animals have similar structures doesn't mean they're related. Bats and birds both have wings and fly, but they are not closely related. They don't share a common ancestor. How did bats and birds both end up with wings? Long ago, the first ancestors of bats and the first ancestors of birds to be born with winglike structures stood a better chance of surviving in their environment than those that did not have these structures. As a result, both bat ancestors and bird ancestors with winglike structures were naturally selected. When organisms that are not related evolve similar structures in order to survive in similar environments, the process is called convergent evolution.

Sometimes natural selection works the other way around. Kangaroos and koalas look very different, but they are closely related. They share a common ancestor that lived millions of years ago. Why do they look so different today? Over many generations and many genetic changes, this ancient ancestor evolved into different kinds of animals. The kangaroo's ancestors evolved powerful legs to travel quickly over wide stretches of land. The koala's ancestors evolved a shape that enables it to climb trees easily. When organisms that are closely related evolve different structures in order to survive in different environments, the process is called adaptive radiation.

◄ Kangaroo

◄ Koala

UNIT 2: HEREDITY, DIVERSITY, AND CHANGE

80

© GREAT SOURCE. COPYING IS PROHIBITED.

Explore

ADAPTIVE RADIATION: SPIDERS All of the 35,000 known species of spiders evolved from a common ancestor that lived many millions of years ago. Through many generations and genetic changes, different kinds of spiders became adapted to different environments.

Look at these photos and facts about two different kinds of spiders, then answer the question below.

▲ **The red-kneed tarantula (*Megaphobema mesomelas*) is large and hairy. It feeds on insects and other spiders.**

The black widow ▶ (*Latrodectus mactans*) is considered the most venomous spider in North America.

▶ *How do the physical adaptations of each spider help it survive?*

Take Action

CONVERGENT EVOLUTION IN THE DESERT Many different species make their home in the Sahara desert of Africa. Some examples include the horned viper, the desert monitor, the desert hedgehog, the elephant shrew, and the barbary leopard. Research three different animals that live in the Sahara. Create a chart that shows how the shape and structure of each animal have adapted for survival in hot, dry, sandy conditions. In what ways are these adaptations similar?

FIND OUT MORE

SCIENCESAURUS

Recognizing Common Ancestors 125
The Theory of Evolution 126

www.scilinks.org
Keyword: Evolution
Code: GSLD12

81

One Hundred Million Kinds of Things

What's in a Name?

A discovery led to a new category of insects.

Scientists use a classification system to identify every known organism on Earth. There are nine categories in the system—domain, kingdom, phylum, class, order, family, genus, species, and subspecies. Domain is the broadest category, and subspecies is the smallest. The classification of one of the most common kinds of honeybees is given in the chart below.

▲Honeybee

The scientific classification system shows how organisms are related. For example, all insects are grouped in the same class, Insecta. This class is divided into smaller groups called orders. All butterflies belong to the same order. All beetles belong to another order.

Honeybee Classification	
Domain	Eukarya
Kingdom	Animalia
Phylum	Arthropoda
Class	Insecta
Order	Hymenoptera
Family	Apidae
Genus	Apis
Species	mellifera
Subspecies	ligustica

When scientists discover a new organism, they must figure out how it fits into the classification system. Finding a new genus or species is not unusual for scientists, but finding a new order or family is a rare and exciting event. In 2002, entomologist Oliver Zompro found an insect that didn't fit into any of the 30 existing orders of insects.

► **Before You Read**

CLASSIFY IT Think of a collection you have—CDs, books, or stamps, for example. Select one of the items in that collection, and classify it according to the scientific categories above. (For example, domain: Recordings; kingdom: CDs; phylum: Music; class: Classical Music, and so on.)

► *If you added a new item to the collection, would it fit easily into your system? Explain.*

_____

_____

_____

Underline the sentences that explain why "the gladiator" did not belong in the same order as stick insects.

Read

Entomologist Oliver Zompro thought a certain insect had been extinct for millions of years. Then he found living specimens in Africa.

New Order of Insects Discovered

For the first time [since 1915], researchers have discovered an insect that constitutes a new order of insects. Dubbed "the gladiator" [for the movie] entomologist Oliver Zompro...said it resembles "a cross between a stick insect, a mantid, and a grasshopper...." The discovery of the new insect order... increases the number of insect orders to 31. "This discovery is [like] finding a mastodon or saber-toothed tiger," said [one scientist].

Zompro, a specialist in stick insects, was studying... fossils...when he began to suspect he was seeing a new type of insect.... When Zompro dissected [one] specimen...he found the remains of insects in its gut.... [This showed] that the stick-like insect was a carnivore. All other known stick-like insects are plant eaters. "At this point, I was sure I had found an absolutely new order of insects," said Zompro. He set out to [see] whether the insect—which [scientists thought was] extinct—might still be found in the wild.

He joined an expedition to [Namibia in Africa].... The scientists were dropped onto a mountain peak in the remote area.... After a night of shaking grass bushes, a scientist... found the first of the live insects that came to be known as "the gladiator." During the trip, Zompro collected a dozen of the insects, which he carried back to his lab...to study....

▲ "The gladiator"

constitutes: makes up
entomologist: a scientist who studies insects
mantid: a large, green insect; one type is known as a "praying mantis"
mastodon: a woolly mammoth, an extinct relative of modern elephants

saber-toothed tiger: a huge lion-like animal, now extinct
specimen: an individual example of an organism
gut: digestive system

From: Trevedi, Bijal P. "New Insect Order Found in Southern Africa." *National Geographic Today.*

FIND OUT MORE

SCIENCESAURUS
Classification   150

83

▶ Explore

COMPARE ORDERS All insects that are classified in the same order share many characteristics. The chart below provides information about the four orders of insects that are mentioned in the reading.

Order	Type of Wings	How It Moves Around	Diet	How It Catches and Holds Its Prey
Gladiators (Mantophasmatodea)	no wings	walks	insects, including other gladiators	uses front and middle pair of legs
Walking sticks (Phasmatodea)	small, useless wings or no wings (most species)	walks	plants	✕
Mantids (Mantodea)	thickened front wings, long hind wings	walks, flies some	insects such as crickets	uses front pair of legs
Grasshoppers (Orthoptera)	thickened front wings protect long, thin hind wings	walks, jumps, flies short distances	plants (most species)	✕

▶ *Examine the characteristics listed in the chart. Which insects besides gladiators are carnivores? Why didn't Zompro classify gladiators in the same order as those insects?*

_____

_____

▶ *Why did Zompro's discovery lead to the creation of a new insect order?*

_____

_____

_____

84

Propose Explanations

An organism's traits are determined by its DNA. Every species has a unique DNA pattern. By comparing DNA patterns, scientists can determine whether one species is related to other species, even species that are now extinct.

▶ *How would comparing the DNA of the gladiator and walking sticks help scientists classify the gladiator?*

_____

_____

_____

_____

Michael Whiting is a biologist doing DNA research on the gladiator. He said, DNA "is one more piece of a large and complex puzzle. It's exciting to have the piece, but it's not going to provide the answer by itself."

▶ *DNA can tell scientists a lot about a species, but not everything. What kinds of information can be learned only by observing a live gladiator in natural surroundings?*

_____

_____

_____

_____

_____

▶ Take Action

INTO THE FIELD Entomologists spend part of their time collecting specimens in the wild to bring back to the lab for more study. With another student, go outside with two small, clear containers with lids (be sure to poke airholes in the lids) and a flat wooden stick or plastic coffee stirrer. Use the stick or stirrer to help place one insect in each jar. (When you are finished observing the insects, return them unharmed to the area where you found them.) Avoid capturing any insects that you think might sting or bite. Take notes to identify features of each insect, such as wings or no wings, coloring, and so on. Use the library or Internet to research the classification of each of the two insects—from its kingdom down through its phylum, class, order, and (if possible) its family.

One Hundred Million Kinds of Things

WE ARE FAMILY

Should giant pandas be classified with bears or with raccoons? Scientists have debated this question for more than 100 years.

The giant panda is famous for its black and white fur and big, bear-shaped body. It spends about 12 hours a day eating. Its diet is made up almost entirely of one food—bamboo. Giant pandas make their home high in the isolated mountain forests of central China. Another species of panda, the red panda, is found in forested mountains of western China. These remote locations make it difficult for scientists to study pandas.

NOTEZONE

Number the different ways that the giant panda has been classified.

> ▶ **Read**

Sometimes, classifying an organism is not so easy.

The "Bear Facts"

One of the world's rarest animals, the giant panda, lives in the subalpine forests in the west central region of China. The classification of the panda has long been a matter of controversy among zoologists. Originally classified with the bears, it was later grouped with raccoons. The weight of evidence that has accumulated over the years, however, now supports the view that it is related to bears. Its closest relative is the spectacled bear of South America.

subalpine: just below the highest places that trees will grow on a mountain

zoologist: a scientist who studies, observes, and classifies animals

From: "Giant Panda," *Canadian Museum of Nature* (www.nature.ca/notebooks/english/gpanda.htm)

FIND OUT MORE

SCIENCESAURUS

Classification
Hierarchy   151

SCILINKS
THE WORLD'S A CLICK AWAY

www.scilinks.org
Keyword: Taxonomy
Code: GSLD13

▲ **Giant panda**

UNIT 2: HEREDITY, DIVERSITY, AND CHANGE

▶ **Explore**

IDENTIFYING FAMILIES Compare the giant panda's characteristics with the characteristics of the other animals listed in the chart.

Appearance and Behavior	Giant panda	Red panda	Raccoon	Spectacled bear
has dark, mask-like fur around eyes	yes	yes	yes	yes
eats bamboo plants	yes	yes	no	no
has long wrist bones covered with skin that function like human thumbs	yes	yes	no	no
has ringed tail pattern	no	yes	yes	no
is bear-like in size and weight	yes	no	no	yes
has bear-like teeth	no	no	yes	yes
can walk on hind legs	no	no	no	yes

▶ *Which of the other animals does the giant panda seem most closely related to? What evidence from the chart led you to that conclusion?*

_____

_____

_____

_____

_____

_____

▶ *The giant panda was first classified in the Ursidae family with bears. During the mid-1900s, it was reclassified in the Procyonidae family with raccoons. What characteristics of the spectacled bear are not shared by giant pandas?*

_____

_____

_____

_____

_____

NEW EVIDENCE, NEW CLASSIFICATION Just when scientists thought the giant panda would remain in the raccoon family, they discovered a new tool to help classify animals—DNA analysis. Scientists assume that closely related animals will have more DNA (genes) in common than animals that are distantly related. By comparing different animals' DNA, scientists can find out about the animals' ancestors.

Scientists analyzed DNA samples from the giant panda, the red panda, the raccoon, and the spectacled bear. They discovered that all four animals have some DNA in common. This meant that they all evolved from one common ancestor in the distant past. But the giant panda and the spectacled bear have more DNA in common with each other than they have in common with the raccoon and red panda. And the red panda and raccoon have more DNA in common with each other than they have in common with the giant panda and spectacled bear. Based on this DNA analysis, scientists developed the "family tree" shown on the next page.

Red pandas

Giant pandas

Raccoons

Bears

Common ancestor to raccoons and red panda

Common ancestor to giant panda and bears

Common ancestor to all

▶ **Why do you think scientists changed the giant panda's classification after they studied its DNA?**

_____

_____

▶ **How is classifying animals based on their physical characteristics different from classifying them based on DNA evidence? Which evidence do you think is more useful to scientists? Explain why.**

_____

_____

_____

_____

_____

_____

_____

One Hundred Million Kinds of Things

It's Classified!

With more than 350 shark species to choose from, identifying one particular shark can be a challenge!

▲ **Caribbean reef shark**

Scientists sometimes use a dichotomous key to help identify organisms. The key presents a series of choices between two characteristics. By choosing one characteristic at each step, they can identify the organism.

▶ **Activity**

SHARK, SHARK! WHO'S THERE?

Eight different shark species are pictured on the next page. Use the dichotomous key below to identify each kind of shark.

What to Do:
Choose one of the shark pictures. Go to step 1 on the key. Decide whether **a** or **b** fits the shark you chose. If **b** fits, go to step 2 on the key. Again, decide which choice fits the shark. Continue through the key until you reach the shark's name. Write the name below the shark's picture. Repeat the steps until you have identified all eight sharks.

DICHOTOMOUS KEY

1	**a.** mouth at front of snout	African angel shark
	b. mouth underneath snout	Go to **2**
2	**a.** no anal fin	Go to **3**
	b. has anal fin	Go to **4**
3	**a.** very long snout	Japanese saw shark
	b. short snout	Cookie-cutter shark
4	**a.** two dorsal fins	Go to **5**
	b. one dorsal fin	Broadnose seven-gill shark
5	**a.** mouth ends in front of eyes	Go to **6**
	b. mouth continues beyond eyes	Go to **7**
6	**a.** barbels (fleshy whiskers) on lower jaw	Nurse shark
	b. no barbels on lower jaw	Whale shark
7	**a.** nictitating eyelid (membrane that moves over eye to protect it)	Smooth hammerhead shark
	b. no nictitating eyelid	Great white shark

UNIT 2: HEREDITY, DIVERSITY, AND CHANGE

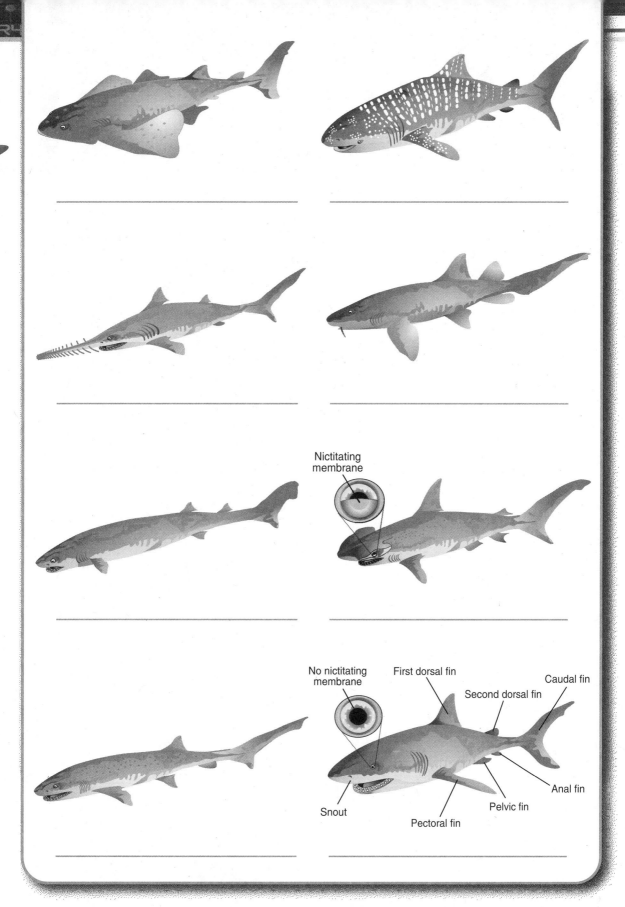

Nictitating
membrane

No nictitating
membrane

First dorsal fin

Second dorsal fin

Caudal fin

Anal fin

Pelvic fin

Pectoral fin

Snout

Living Things

All living things on Earth come into contact with other living things.

That's when it gets interesting for scientists who study these relationships. They observe things such as how insects can get to plants they can eat, and how plants catch insects they can eat.

I n this unit, you'll learn how organisms—from bacteria to bugs to birds—get around and interact with each other. Sometimes when two organisms interact, it's a little like a fight; one must harm the other in order to survive. Other times, such as when a bird eats a plant's seeds and drops them somewhere else, both organisms benefit. You'll also learn how insects escape certain interactions and how whales interact with other whales in their groups.

THE CHAPTERS IN THIS UNIT ARE . . .

CHAPTER 9:
Bacteria
Find out: How many different kinds of bacteria have been found living on dollar bills?

CHAPTER 10:
How Insects Get Around
Find out: How fast does a flea beetle travel when it jumps?

CHAPTER 11:
Killer Whales: Wolves of the Sea
Find out: How do scientists tell one killer whale from another?

CHAPTER 12:
Plant Adaptations
Find out: Can a plant be a predator?

? Did You Know?
Killer whales, especially juveniles, are known to "play." They sometimes chase one another, swim in the wakes of boats, and do tricks in the air. They've even been seen tossing around seabirds and sting rays.

Bacteria

More Bacteria for Your Buck

Should you be washing your money as well as your hands?

All bacteria have just one cell and are some of the smallest forms of life on Earth. Where can you find bacteria? Just about everywhere. One group of researchers found that even the dollar bills that most people carry around with them are perfect homes for all kinds of bacteria. The bills—and the bacteria—travel from person to person with every purchase, and some of these germs are even quite dangerous!

▶ **Before You Read**

THINK ABOUT IT Did your parents ever warn you not to play with money when you were little? "Don't put that near your mouth. You don't know where it's been!" People usually worry about coins because they often fall on the ground. But as you know, money comes in two varieties. The surface of coins is hard and smooth, while bills are soft and somewhat rough.

▶ *Do you think more bacteria live on dollar bills or on coins? Why?*

_____

_____

_____

_____

_____

_____

_____

▶ **Read**

Here is what researchers found in the cracks and crevices of your cash.

Dirty Money

Dollar bills support a rich flora of bacteria, some of them infectious, say research physicians Theodore W. Pope and Peter T. Ender of the Medical Center of Wright-Patterson Air Force Base in Ohio.

They worked with Michael A. Koroscil at Beavercreek (Ohio) High School, who originated the idea for a science-fair project. The group counted the [kinds of] bacteria living on 68 dollar bills collected from people in line at a high school sporting event and a grocery store.

The researchers incubated each bill in nutrient broth for up to a day and then grew any bacteria in culture dishes to identify them. More than half the bills hosted bacteria that commonly infect people in hospitals or those who have depressed immune systems, the team reported. Five of the bills contained a bacterium that can sicken healthy people, either *Klebsiella pneumonia* [which causes pneumonia] or *Staphylococcus aureus* [which can cause deadly infections]. The researchers identified a total of 93 different types of bacteria living on the bills, and two-thirds of the bills had at least one type.

▲ **Bacteria growing in culture dish**

---

flora: a group of plants, bacteria, or other microorganisms
infectious: capable of spreading disease
incubated: maintained a precise temperature or other conditions so organisms could develop
nutrient broth: a "soup" of substances used to feed organisms
culture dish: a dish used to hold tiny organisms while they grow
hosted: made a home or provided space for organisms
depressed: weakened

FIND OUT MORE

SCIENCESAURUS

Cells	076
Immune System	098
Kingdom Monera	157

SCI LINKS
THE WORLD'S A CLICK AWAY

www.scilinks.org
Keyword: Bacteria
Code: GSLD14

From: Netting, Jessica. "Dirty Money Harbors Bacterial Dangers." *Science News.*

WHAT BACTERIA NEED Because paper money is woven, it offers plenty of nooks and crannies where bacteria can make their homes.

▶ *Name three other objects in your home that have tiny crevices where bacteria could grow.*

_____

_____

Like all living things, bacteria also need water to survive. Paper absorbs moisture from the air or objects around it—another reason bacteria thrive on dollar bills.

▶ *Would the three objects you named also provide moisture for bacteria? If not, name three other objects in your home that would provide a moist environment for bacteria.*

_____

_____

Bacteria also need nutrients to survive. This is why food spoils—bacteria are making both a meal and a home of the food. Bacteria can get their nutrients from many sources. It might be from the same things that we eat, or from the things we throw away, from the skin oil on our hands, or even from our waste products.

▶ *Protected places, water, and nutrients—these are the three things that bacteria need. Knowing this, where do you think would be the best places to find bacteria in your home? List three.*

_____

_____

▶ **Propose Explanations**

GERMY MONEY

▶ *Why do you think the researchers were so interested in studying the bacteria on dollar bills? Why would bacteria that live on money be more dangerous to people than bacteria that live inside your sneakers, for example?*

_____

_____

_____

The bacteria that live on paper money are usually not a great threat to our health. However, over 50 percent of the bills in the research study carried bacteria that could cause disease. Even so, most people do not get sick from handling paper money. The people most at risk are those who are already sick or who have a weakened immune system.

▶ *Why do most people stay healthy after handling money? Why are the bacteria on paper money more dangerous to people who are already sick?*

_____

_____

_____

_____

_____

▶ *Describe ways that we can avoid spreading germs on dollar bills.*

_____

_____

_____

HEALTH IS WEALTH Using what you've learned about bacteria, design a new type of money to replace dollar bills. The new money should not give bacteria a good place to live and grow. Draw your new money and explain why it would avoid the problems of paper money.

Bacteria

THE BAD GUYS

These guys are small, but deadly!

Some bacteria are deadly. One of the best known is *Yersinia pestis*, the bacterium responsible for the bubonic plague, or "Black Death" as it was commonly called. Over the course of history, bubonic plague has killed hundreds of millions of people around the world.

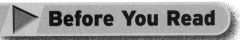

▶ Before You Read

Microscopic view of *Yersinia pestis* bacteria

MAKE A PREDICTION One way humans get the bacterium that causes bubonic plague is from the bite of a flea that usually lives on rats. The bubonic plague spread across the world in A.D. 540.

▶ *How do you think it could have traveled from one continent to another?*

_____

_____

_____

_____

▶ Read

NOTEZONE

Underline the
places where
the plague
broke out in
A.D. 540 and
first spread.
Use a world
map to find
those places
and mark
them on
the map on
page 98.

Here is how one of the smallest life forms wiped out entire populations of people.

KILLER GERMS

The bubonic form [of the plague] is characterized by large buboes, [which are] swollen lymph nodes in the neck, armpits or groin.... Bubonic plague victims characteristically flex and extend their arms in attempts to lessen the pain of the buboes. Infection of the blood can lead to bleeding beneath the skin, which causes the characteristic black splodges on the skin. These symptoms are accompanied by a very high fever, headache, shaking chills, and delirium and are followed by death in fifty to sixty percent of cases when left untreated.

...In A.D. 540, during the reign of Emperor Justinian, a pandemic (an epidemic that spreads across whole continents) broke out in Pelusium, Lower Egypt, and spread throughout Alexandria and on to Palestine. From there it traveled the world. At the peak of the crisis, estimates suggest that ten thousand people were dying each day. Maybe one hundred million people died in all. Historians say this scourge contributed to the fall of the Roman Empire.

---

lymph nodes: small structures in the body that remove and kill bacteria and other microorganisms
flex: bend
extend: straighten
splodges: patches or large, uneven spots
delirium: mental confusion
scourge: a source of widespread suffering

From: Moore, Pete. *Killer Germs: Rogue Diseases of the Twenty-First Century.* Carlton Books Limited 2001.

Rat ▶

HOW THE PLAGUE TRAVELS Deadly bacteria often travel through animals before reaching human beings. The first organisms bubonic plague bacteria infect are fleas that live on rats. The bacteria do not kill the fleas. When the infected fleas bite the rats, they pass the bacteria to them, and soon the rats die. If the fleas cannot find another rat, they may then move to a human and bring the deadly bacteria with them.

▶ *Suggest some ways that people could keep the plague from spreading.*

_____

_____

_____

_____

_____

▶ *Draw a diagram to show how Yersinia pestis bacteria usually travel to humans.*

▲ Flea viewed with a microscope.

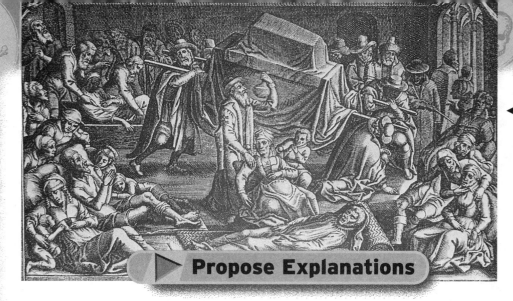

◄ Plague victims in an engraving by J. Orlers, 1674

▶ Propose Explanations

THINK ABOUT IT In 1665 the Black Death attacked London and killed about one third of the city's population of 500,000 before dying out.

▶ *What do you think would have happened to Yersinia pestis bacteria if the plague had wiped out the entire city?*

_____

_____

_____

▶ *The plague often spread in cities. What is it about cities that makes them such good homes for infectious bacteria? What are some of the ways you can protect yourself from bacteria wherever you live?*

_____

_____

_____

▶ Take Action

GERM-INATE AWARENESS Bubonic plague is no longer a major health threat. Cities today are cleaner, and doctors can recognize plague symptoms quickly and treat the disease with antibiotics.

However, other infectious diseases caused by bacteria do threaten humans today. Choose one such infectious disease to research. Some examples are food poisoning, Lyme disease, staph infections, tuberculosis, and typhus. Find out how the disease is transmitted to people, what the symptoms are, where the disease is most common, and how to prevent it from spreading. Present your findings on a poster or in a brief oral report.

Bacteria

Bacteria at Work

Is "bacteria" just another word for disease? Not at all!

Most of the bacteria we hear about are harmful to humans, but that's just because bad guys always make the headlines. Most bacteria are not harmful to us at all. There are many different kinds of bacteria living inside our bodies that help keep us healthy.

Bacteria in yogurt

▶ **Read**

A 13-year-old student named Rachel wrote an essay about bacteria and won the Young Naturalist Award from the American Museum of Natural History for her work.

BACTERIA GOOD GUYS

Bacteria are responsible for much more than just diseases. There are thousands of kinds of bacteria. Most of them are harmless to humans.

Vast numbers of bacteria live in our bodies. One example is found in the intestine. The bacteria help us with digestion and to produce vitamins. In exchange, they soak up a little extra food for themselves. Neat. Huh? Most dairy products are made by or with the help of bacteria. Some dairy foods are cheese, buttermilk, yogurt, and sour cream. Some other kinds of foods that involve bacteria in their production are pickles and high fructose corn syrup. Can you imagine our soda without high fructose corn syrup? A hamburger with no cheese or pickles?

Bacteria are very important in medicine. Doctors and scientists have figured out how to use dead or weakened bacteria to prevent other bacterial diseases. This process is called vaccination. Vaccination has helped us all become a lot healthier than we were a hundred years ago.... Bacteria do so much for us, where would we be without them?

fructose: a sugar found in fruit and honey

From: Mock, Rachel. "Bacteria." *Young Naturalist Awards.* American Museum of Natural History. (www.amnh.org/nationalcenter/youngnaturalistawards/1998/bacteria.html)

NOTEZONE

What else would you like to know about helpful bacteria in our bodies?

FIND OUT MORE

SCIENCESAURUS
Kingdom Monera 157
Renewable Material Resources 330

UNIT 3: LIVING THINGS

102

▶ Explore

"GOOD" OR "BAD"? Bacteria are doing the same thing we're doing—trying to stay alive. Unfortunately, what some bacteria do to stay alive means harm to us. For example, some bacteria that cause food to spoil do not harm people. But when those bacteria break down food, they give off chemicals that are poisonous to us. However, there are also bacteria that help us while they help themselves, such as the bacteria in our intestines. Bacteria are also what turn milk into yogurt and cabbage into sauerkraut. One scientist has even found sewer bacteria that release a gas that may someday be able to be used as a fuel!

▶ *Is there really such a thing as "good" bacteria and "bad" bacteria? Why do we call bacteria "good" or "bad"?*

_____

_____

_____

▶ Propose Explanations

HELPFUL BACTERIA A group of scientists did an experiment using the following hypothesis: A daily dose of certain intestinal bacteria may keep children who are in hospitals from getting diarrhea so they won't have to spend extra time in the hospital. The diarrhea is usually caused by a virus that the children catch while they are in the hospital.

   The scientists tested their hypothesis by giving one group of children a dose of beneficial bacteria called *Lactobaccillus GG* twice a day during their hospital stay. Another group was given a placebo, a pill that doesn't have any effect. The scientists found that the risk of getting diarrhea was 80 percent lower in the group that received the bacteria than in the group that didn't.

▶ *Based on what you know about "good" intestinal bacteria, suggest a possible reason for these results.*

_____

_____

_____

_____

_____

How Insects Get Around

Walk Like an Insect

Walking seems easy, but what if you had six legs?

There are more kinds of insects than any other kind of animal on Earth. Scientists have identified about 800,000 species of insects, and they know that there are many more yet to be found!

All adult insects have a body made up of three parts, with six legs attached to the middle part. Beyond that, insects are very different. One way insects differ from each other is in how they get around. Many insects get around just by walking on their six legs. That's a lot of legs to coordinate!

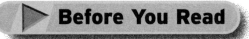

▶ **Before You Read**

HOW DO THEY DO IT? We all know how people with two legs walk—after all, most do it every day. One leg goes forward, then the other, then the first leg again, and so on. But how does a six-legged insect walk? By moving one leg at a time? All three on one side and then all three on the other?

Find out what method works best by teaming up with two classmates to form a six-legged "insect." Stand one in front of the other, and put your hands on the shoulders of the person in front of you.

▶ *Now try to get your "insect" to move forward. First try to walk without talking to your "other legs." Then try planning with your teammates how you will move. What did you learn?*

_____

_____

_____

_____

_____

_____

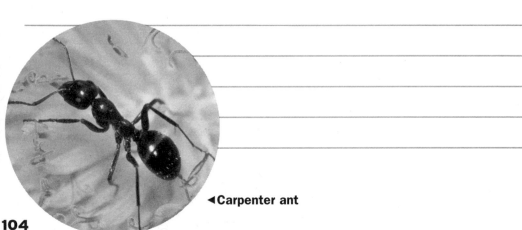

◀**Carpenter ant**

UNIT 3: LIVING THINGS

▶ Read

NOTEZONE

(Circle) all the phrases that describe insect actions.

Amazingly, insects are able to move their six legs without ever getting them tangled. Here's how they do it.

Insect March

Insects have six multi-jointed legs that make them very stable. They can start fast and stop suddenly without falling over. They are also very light, making it easy for them to maneuver....

When an insect walks, it moves three legs at a time. The first and third legs on one side and the middle leg on the other side all step forward together. Then it's the turn of the other three legs to step out. The end result is a slightly zigzagging walk.

----

multi-jointed: having many places that bend

stable: steady and hard to throw off balance

maneuver: change direction and position

From: Robertson, Matthew. *Reader's Digest Pathfinders: Insects and Spiders.* Reader's Digest Children's Publishing, Inc.

▼ **Click beetle**

▶ Explore

SHAKE A LEG! Get together again with your insect teammates. Stand in a line as you did before. Now try to walk the way real insects walk. Try walking across the room in a straight path.

▶ *Descibe the path you made across the room. Explain what happened when you tried to walk in a straight line. Why do you think a single insect walks more easily than three two-legged people walking together?*

_____

_____

_____

_____

FIND OUT MORE

SCIENCESAURUS

Structure and
    Function   075
Vertebrates and
    Invertebrates   161

SCILINKS.
THE WORLD'S A CLICK AWAY

www.scilinks.org
Keyword: Insects
Code: GSLD15

▶*How does walking help an insect survive? List three things an insect needs to do to survive that walking helps it do.*

_____

_____

_____

_____

▶*How does the structure of an insect allow it to walk and therefore survive?*

_____

_____

_____

_____

_____

▶*Think of a situation where an insect's six legs do not help it survive.*

_____

_____

_____

_____

▶ Propose Explanations

DON'T KNOCK ME OVER When most of an object's mass is near the ground, it is said to have a low center of gravity. Objects that have a low center of gravity are harder to knock over than objects whose center of gravity is higher. Legs that are spaced far apart also help.

▶*Identify two things that help make an insect's body stable.*

_____

_____

_____

_____

▶Now look at the following insects. Which one do you think is the most stable when it walks? Explain how that insect's structure makes it more stable than the other insects.

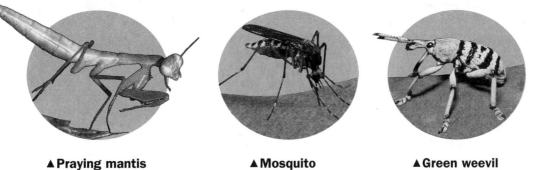

▲Praying mantis   ▲Mosquito   ▲Green weevil

_____

_____

_____

_____

▶Imagine an insect walking along a tree branch in the wind. How does being stable help the insect survive in these conditions?

_____

_____

_____

Take Action

WALK THE WALK Imagine that you work at a science museum in the Hall of Insects. It's your job to explain to visitors how an insect walks. How could you show which legs move when? Draw and label a diagram of an insect's footprints as it walks.

How Insects Get Around

Jump!

Why walk when jumping gets you there so much faster?

Have you ever tried to catch a grasshopper, only to have it jump away? Grasshoppers can walk, but mostly they jump. Many other insects that can do both also jump more than walk. Why? They can travel faster by jumping. Traveling faster makes the insect better able to escape a predator. For fleas, jumping is the best way to quickly get from the ground onto the body of a passing animal, where it will find food and shelter.

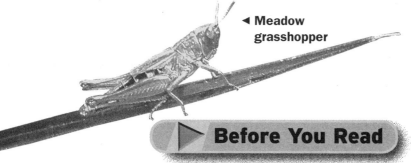

◄ **Meadow grasshopper**

▶ **Before You Read**

JUMPING GEAR Many animals have special body parts that allow them to "spring into action."

▶ *Make a list of animals that can jump. What body parts do they have that are specially adapted for jumping? How is jumping helpful to each animal's survival? Draw and describe your ideas below.*

NOTEZONE

Circle all the words related to structures that help insects jump.

Read

Jumping is a good way to go—and there's more than one way to do it!

Leaping Insects

Some [insect] species...have developed [body parts] made just for jumping. Grasshoppers have such powerful back legs that they can make leaps many times higher than their bodies. Some jumpers don't use legs at all—tiny springtails flick a special "tail," while click beetles use a peg-like spring to propel themselves....

When [the] flea beetle makes a jump, it shoots through the air at speeds greater than 9 miles [14km] per hour, spinning head-over-claws 70 times in a single second. [And it] still manages to land feet first. The enlarged back legs hold a special jumping [muscle]...that lets the beetle leap at such speeds and always land where it wants.

propel: move forward

From: Robertson, Matthew. *Reader's Digest Pathfinders: Insects and Spiders*. Reader's Digest Children's Publishing, Inc.

Propose Explanations

AT HOME IN THE GRASS Grasshoppers live among tall grasses. Eating grass and other plants gives grasshoppers energy. Moving uses energy. It takes less energy for the grasshopper to jump than it does for it to walk the same distance because it has specially adapted back legs.

▶ *How might jumping help the grasshopper survive in its environment?*

FIND OUT MORE

SCIENCESAURUS
Structure and
Function   075

How Insects Get Around

Flights of Fancy

Look! Up in the sky! What is it? A bird? A plane? No, it's a dragonfly!

Imagine that you're sitting by a pond on a warm summer day. If you look along the surface of the water, you'll notice many different kinds of insects moving around. Some seem to be floating in the air. But others, such as dragonflies, are expert fliers that can do amazing acrobatics.

The book *A Dragon in the Sky* tells the story of a male green darner dragonfly named Anax that lives in the northeastern U.S. The name Anax comes from the scientific name of the green darner dragonfly, *Anax junius*. Anax's two pairs of wings move independently, allowing him to fly expertly. Like the other green darners in his area, Anax will migrate to areas in the southern state of Florida when the weather gets colder.

 **Before You Read**

MIGRATION Most animals move around for several hours each day as they search for food, water, shelter, and mates. Some animals go on even longer journeys called migrations. Some animals migrate to better feeding grounds every summer, others to a watering hole every dry season, still others to a warmer place in winter. Other animals make only one migration in their lifetime—a journey to where they will lay their eggs and then die.

▶ *Which animals can you think of that migrate? Where do they go? Do they fly, walk, or swim? What benefit do you think they gain from migrating? Record that information in the chart below.*

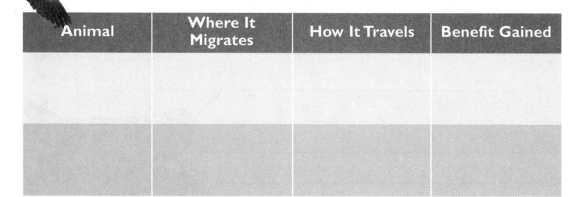

Animal	Where It Migrates	How It Travels	Benefit Gained

▶ **Read**

NOTEZONE

What did
Anax do to
prepare for
his migration?

Like all dragonflies, Anax can fly with great skill.

FLIGHT OF THE DRAGONFLY

His wings were strong but flexible. They could not only beat up and down but also twist and bend.... Fine hairs on the upper surface of Anax's wings measured the airflow. His eyes kept track of his surroundings, including the horizon. All of this information was sent to his brain. Without thinking, Anax made dozens of changes in his wing and body positions every minute....

Anax could hover in midair, then beat all four wings together and, in a few seconds, accelerate to thirty miles [48 km] per hour. He could dart to the side, fly backward for a short distance, and even turn an aerial somersault. Flying swiftly, he could stop in an instant by lowering his abdomen and hind legs....

▲ **Green darner dragonfly**

Now [Anax] sensed it was time for a change. He was not yet a fully developed [dragonfly], but he was ready to begin migration. One morning in late September, Anax ate several mosquitoes and a robber fly.... Then he lifted into the air and began to fly south.

airflow: the flow of air over a surface
horizon: the line where Earth and sky appear to meet

accelerate: speed up
aerial: in the air
abdomen: the rear body section of an insect

From: Pringle, Laurence. *A Dragon in the Sky: The Story of a Green Darner Dragonfly.* Orchard Books, a Division of Scholastic, Inc.

FIND OUT MORE

SCIENCESAURUS

Animal Life Cycles 106
Behavior 109
Animal Behavior 110

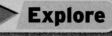
ADAPTED FOR FLIGHT An adaptation is a characteristic that enables an organism to survive in its environment. Flying is one adaptation that helps insects like the dragonfly survive.

▶ *Many body structures must work together for an insect to fly. Label the drawing to explain how Anax's body structures coordinate so he can fly.*

▶ *Herbivores are animals that eat plants. Carnivores are animals that eat other animals. Are dragonflies herbivores or carnivores? How can you tell?*

_____

_____

▶ *Think about a time you tried to slap a mosquito. Do you think mosquitoes would be easy for a predator to catch? Explain.*

_____

_____

▶ *How does a dragonfly's flying skill make it a successful predator?*

_____

_____

▶ *What environmental change triggered Anax's migration?*

_____

_____

DESCRIBING CHARACTER When writers create a story, they sometimes use anthropomorphism to make the story's characters more interesting. *Anthropomorphism* means describing animals or objects as having human feelings, thoughts, and reasons for doing things.

▶ *Review the reading in this lesson. Is the description of Anax an example of anthropomorphism? Why or why not?*

_____

_____

_____

_____

Recall a story you enjoyed when you were young that was about the make-believe adventures of an animal or object. *The Little Engine That Could, Corduroy,* and *The Three Little Pigs* are three examples. Write two or three sentences from the story that use anthropomorphism to describe the nonhuman characters. Then rewrite each sentence so it is not anthropomorphic.

_____

_____

_____

_____

_____

_____

_____

_____

_____

_____

_____

_____

_____

Sounds of the Sea

If you were a killer whale, how would you stay in touch with other killer whales?

Killer whales are found in all oceans of the world. The groups we know the most about are found along the west coast of North America. That's where killer whale biologist John Ford and his colleagues conduct their studies about whale biology and behavior. Scientists know that killer whales form groups called pods in which they live and hunt. They also know that a pod of whales can be a noisy group.

 **Before You Read**

NOISY WHALES Whale biologists have recorded a wide variety of sounds made by killer whales under water.

▶ *Why do you think the whales make sounds? What functions do you think the sounds serve?*

_____

_____

_____

_____

_____

_____

> **Read**

Whale biologist John Ford has discovered a lot about the different sounds that killer whales make under water.

CLICKS, CALLS, AND WHISTLES

Killer whales rely heavily on underwater sound for both navigation and communication, and with good reason. Sound is by far the most efficient and reliable [way to collect] sensory information about a whale's surroundings and for social communication with other whales....

The echolocation signals produced by the whales are [called] "click trains," which are short-duration pulses given in [repeated] series that may last for 10 seconds or more. Echoes from these clicks allow the animals to form an acoustical image of their surroundings....

The signals used for social communication within and between pods consist of calls and whistles. Calls are more common than whistles.... Typically less than two seconds long, calls are made up of bursts and pulses [produced] at rates of up to several thousand per second. Such pulse bursts produce high-pitched squeals and screams, not unlike the sounds made by rusty hinges on a quickly closing door. By varying the timing and [pitch]...of these bursts, the whales can generate a variety of complex signals.... These calls appear to serve generally as contact signals, coordinating group behavior and keeping pod members in touch when they are out of sight of each other....

navigation: finding one's way
efficient: getting the best result for the least amount of effort
reliable: dependable
sensory: related to sight, hearing, and the other senses

echolocation: a system of using bounced sounds to determine the location of objects
short-duration: lasting for a short amount of time
acoustical: related to sound
pitch: how high or low a sound is

From: Ford, John K.B., Graeme M. Ellis, and Kenneth C. Balcomb. *Killer Whales.* UBC Press.

NOTEZONE

What are the functions of clicks and calls in echolocation?

FIND OUT MORE

SCIENCESAURUS
Animal Behavior 110

SCiLINKS
THE WORLD'S A CLICK AWAY

www.scilinks.org
Keyword: Whales
Code:GSLD16

115

NAVIGATING UNDER WATER The following diagram shows how echolocation works. The lines represent sound waves. Sound waves move away from their source and spread out in all directions. When the sound waves hit an object, they bounce off and travel back to the source.

▶ *Look at the diagram. Explain how the killer whale uses sound waves to locate an object.*

_____

_____

_____

_____

▶ *How do you think the killer whale can tell the direction of the object?*

_____

_____

_____

▶ *How do you think the killer whale can tell how far away the object is?*

_____

_____

_____

_____

THINK ABOUT IT

▶ *What do most land mammals use to navigate?*

_____

_____

Bats, which hunt at night, also use echolocation. But both bats and whales have eyes.

▶ *Why do you suppose killer whales and bats use echolocation instead of sight to find their way?*

_____

_____

▶ *Think about common land mammals, such as squirrels, dogs, and cats. What do most land mammals use to communicate?*

_____

_____

▶ *Communication helps killer whales survive in their environment. How might communicating with other members of its pod help a killer whale survive?*

_____

_____

_____

_____

_____

▶ Take Action

PET PROJECT Do you have a pet at home? If not, maybe a close friend has one. Think about how the animal communicates with members of its own species and with people. How does it communicate? What parts of its body does it use? How does it combine sounds and movements to get its message across? What do you think it is trying to communicate? How does communicating help the animal? How well can a person understand the pet's messages?

▶ *Record your ideas and observations on a separate sheet of paper. Make a drawing that shows how the animal communicates.*

Killer Whales: Wolves of the Sea

The Hunters

If you're a killer whale, your choice could be teamwork or going hungry.

Killer whales are not really whales at all. They are classified as members of the dolphin family. However, dolphins and whales are closely related. Early fishermen who watched killer whales hunt and kill whales called them "whale killers." But over time, the words were reversed and the animals came to be known as "killer whales." But killer whales hunt more than just whales. They also eat seals, sea lions, and porpoises.

 **Before You Read**

ORGANIZING INFORMATION Like other predators, killer whales hunt for their food. Different animals have different ways of hunting and catching their prey.

▶ *Think of a predator you know of. How does the animal hunt? Does it hunt alone or in a group? Is its prey bigger or smaller than it is, or the same size? Record your ideas below.*

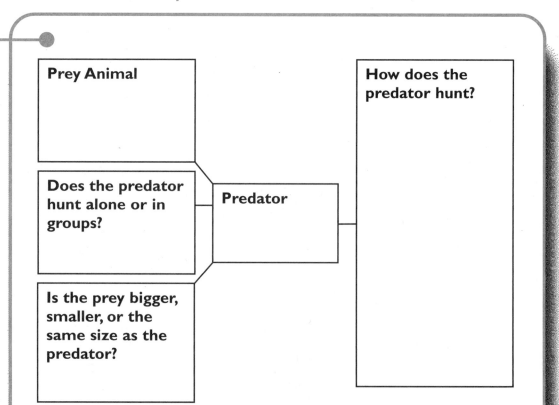

▶ Read

NOTEZONE

What else
would you
like to know
about what
happened
during this
whale hunt?

Michael Bigg, a pioneer of modern killer whale
research, recalls the day he watched a group of killer
whales attack a sea lion.

An Encounter

The sea lion slowly made his way toward the shore
about 200 yards [189 m] away. The [killer] whales were
not concerned by our presence and continued to search
for him. Suddenly, when the sea lion was about 100
yards [91 m] from shore, the whales apparently detected
him with their sonar. They dove in unison, accelerating
toward him. We saw nothing for about 30 seconds,
then the water exploded around him. One after
another, the whales charged the sea lion,
diving around, under, and over him, smashing
him from below and above with their flukes,
and ramming him with their heads. Despite
this fearsome assault, the sea lion
resurfaced every minute or so and
continued his slow progress toward shore.
The episode lasted about 10 minutes in
all. When the sea lion was within
about 50 feet [15 m] of shore, the
whales abruptly abandoned him and
headed rapidly northward.

FIND OUT MORE

SCIENCESAURUS
Animal Behavior   110

sonar: an echolocation system
in unison: all together
accelerating: speeding up
flukes: the two flattened parts
of a whale's tail
assault: attack
episode: event
abandoned: left

Killer whale ▶

From: Ford, John K.B., Graeme M. Ellis. *Transients: Mammal-Hunting Killer Whales.*
UBC Press

WORKING TOGETHER

▶ *How did the killer whales cooperate when they attacked the sea lion?*

_____

_____

▶ *How might hunting in a group help make an attack like this successful?*

_____

_____

_____

▶ *Do you think a single killer whale might have been more successful attacking the sea lion? Why or why not?*

_____

_____

_____

A FORMIDABLE FOE Harbor seals and stellar sea lions are two prey animals that killer whales hunt for food. Study the information in the table. Notice the differences between harbor seals and sea lions.

Predator Species	Weight	Features
Killer whales	up to 5,443 kg	large, cone-shaped teeth
Prey Species	**Weight**	**Features**
Harbor seals	up to 115 kg	no large canine teeth
Stellar sea lions	up to 1,000 kg	large canine teeth

A single killer whale can chase a harbor seal, grab it in its mouth, and eat it.

▶ *Why can't killer whales use this hunting method with sea lions? Why is a group attack better?*

_____

_____

_____

_____

Propose Explanations

WHALE GROUPS Killer whales that hunt sea lions and other marine mammals usually travel together in pods of three, four, or five whales. Killer whales that feed on fish travel together in much larger pods—20 or more whales. Whales that feed on fish do not need to cooperate to attack the fish.

▶ *How might being in a larger pod make cooperative hunting more difficult?*

_____

_____

_____

A behavioral adaptation is something an animal does that helps it survive.

▶ *How does cooperative hunting help some killer whales survive?*

_____

_____

Take Action

GROUP BEHAVIOR Whale biologists have identified two major types of killer whale social groups. One group is called "transients," which means "move from place to place." The other is called "residents," which means "stay in the same place." These terms refer to the types of pods killer whales form and where they live in the ocean. Research the social structure and feeding habits of each type of group. How do they differ? How is each type of social structure suited to the group's feeding habits?

_____

_____

_____

_____

_____

_____

_____

_____

Killer Whales: Wolves of the Sea

Name That Whale

How can you identify an animal that spends most of its life under water?

Usually, killer whales are completely under water. But like other marine mammals, killer whales must come to the surface to breathe air. They can also come up out of the water while they play and hunt. As the whales swim near the water's surface, whale biologists make observations of their behavior and movements. The more information biologists can gather about the whales' behavior, the better they can understand and protect them.

NOTEZONE

Circle the physical characteristics used to identify individual killer whales.

▶ **Read**

Whale researcher Michael Bigg developed a system that all scientists can use to identify individual killer whales.

SNAPSHOT ID

In 1970, Mike Bigg took on the task of determining the population status and dynamics of killer whales in British Columbia.... Early in his study, Mike Bigg devised a technique that would become by far the most important tool in the field research on killer whales—photographic identification of individuals. Mike determined that every whale could be positively identified from naturally occurring nicks and scars on its dorsal fin and the grey "saddle patch" at the base of the fin. By photographing and cataloging every whale, the population could be accurately counted, rather than just estimated, and other important [facts about the whales'] life history could be documented.

status: the condition of a thing
dynamics: movements and changes
dorsal fin: the fin on a whale's back

cataloging: classifying according to an organized system
documented: supported with evidence

From: Ford, John K.B., Graeme M. Ellis. *Transients: Mammal-Hunting Killer Whales.* UBC Press.

► Activity

WHALE IDENTIFICATION Look at the pictures of dorsal fins below. What features could be used to identify each whale?

Give each whale a name based on the unique physical characteristics of its dorsal fin. Write the name below the whale's picture.

► Explore

FIELD TECHNIQUES Whale biologists give each whale a code that tells when it was identified, what pod the whale is in, and whether it was the offspring of another whale in the pod.

► *Why might it be important for all whale observers to use the same system of identification?*

_____

_____

_____

► *What do you think scientists can learn about whale populations by tracking and studying individuals?*

_____

_____

_____

_____

Plant Adaptations

Mistletoe, Birds, and Trees

Mistletoe plant growing on a tree ▼

Mistletoe plants have symbiotic relationships with both birds and trees.

When one organism affects the survival of another organism, scientists say the organisms have a symbiotic relationship. The word *symbiosis* means "living together." Three types of symbiotic relationships are mutualism, parasitism, and commensalism. In mutualistic relationships, both organisms benefit from their interaction with each other. In parasitic relationships, one organism benefits from the interaction while the other is harmed. In commensal relationships, one organism benefits while the other organism is not helped or harmed.

▶ **Before You Read**

WORKING TOGETHER Three symbiotic relationships are described below. Decide if each one is an example of parasitism, mutualism, or commensalism.

▶ *Clownfish live among sea anemones. The anemone's stinging tentacles protect the clownfish from predators. The clownfish cleans the anemone's tentacles by eating material that clings to them.*

_____

▶ *Fleas bite a dog's skin and feed on its blood. Many dogs are allergic to flea saliva, which irritates their skin.*

_____

▶ *Ivy grows up the trunk of a tree. The ivy receives more sunlight high in the tree. The ivy does not take anything from the tree or block the tree's leaves from light.*

_____

124

▶ Read

As the mistletoe bird flies from tree to tree, it spreads the mistletoe's seeds.

The Sticky Seeds of the Mistletoe

The mistletoe bird on the tree branch has something hanging from its rear end. What is it? An odd little white packet, dangling by threads. The bird seems to know the hanger-on is there. It rubs its bottom against the branch and the thing comes off. Now it's stuck on the branch! But the sticky threads remain attached to the bird, stretching out as the bird hops away. Finally they break and the bird is free.

The mistletoe bird will go through this undignified procedure many times a day. Every day. The little package that was stuck to its hind end was a mistletoe seed.... The sticky threads and the constant wiping are the price the bird must pay for the tasty seeds [inside the mistletoe berries] that it loves.

For the wiped-off seeds, life is just beginning. The seed is now in a prime location to begin its vicious attack on the tree!

---

undignified: not respectable; embarrassing

hind: rear

prime: top quality

From: Kneidel, Sally. *Skunk Cabbage, Sundew Plants & Strangler Figs: And 18 More Of The Strangest Plants On Earth.* John Wiley & Sons, Inc.

NOTEZONE

The second sentence in the reading asks what the white packet is. Underline the sentence that answers the question.

▼ **Mistletoe birds**

FIND OUT MORE

SCIENCESAURUS
Natural Selection 127
Relationships Between
Populations 132

www.scilinks.org
Keyword: Adaptation of Plants
Code: GSLD17

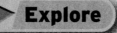

▶ Explore

GIVE AND TAKE When a mistletoe plant blooms, birds feed on the sweet nectar inside the flowers. The plant benefits from this interaction, too. As the bird goes from flower to flower feeding on nectar, it scatters the mistletoe's pollen. This enables the plants to reproduce.

When a bird transfers mistletoe seeds to a tree, the seeds' roots grow into the tree. The new mistletoe plants take water and nutrients from the tree. This can weaken the tree but usually doesn't kill it.

USE GRAPHIC ORGANIZERS Create a graphic organizer that explains all the symbiotic relationships between mistletoe plants, the birds that feed on mistletoe berries, and the trees that the mistletoe plants grow on. Identify each relationship as parasitic, mutualistic, or commensal.

USING GRAPHS Since the mid-1800s, several species of mistletoe in New Zealand have been decreasing in number. Dr. Dave Kelly and his team of scientists investigated the cause for this decline. They found that there is nothing wrong with the mistletoe plants. But over the years, people introduced predators into the region, including cats and rats. The scientists hypothesized that these predators kill the birds that spread the mistletoe's seeds and pollen. Gradually, the number of birds is decreasing. However, from one year to the next, the number of birds does not change very much.

In the 1990s, Dr. Kelly's team studied the number of mistletoe berries produced each year. During the first season, 1994–1995, scientists pollinated the mistletoe plants by hand. This tested whether the mistletoe plants were able to reproduce. During the second season, 1995–1996, the mistletoe was left to be pollinated naturally.

The bar graph below shows the number of mistletoe berries produced during the first two years of their study.

New Zealand Mistletoe

▶ *The number of birds that visited the mistletoe flowers stayed about the same in both seasons. Why do you think there was such a difference in the number of berries that were produced?*

_____

_____

_____

▶ **Do you think this experiment supports the scientists' hypothesis about why the number of mistletoe plants have decreased? Why or why not? How could you improve the experiment to make the results more accurate? Explain your answer.**

_____

_____

_____

_____

MAKE A PREDICTION Using what you know about mutualistic relationships, what is a possible outcome if the number of birds that feed on mistletoe in the area continues to decline? Explain your answer.

_____

_____

Plant Adaptations

NOT YOUR USUAL CARNIVORES

Venus flytrap ▶
(Dionaea muscipula)

Not enough nutrients in the soil? That's no problem if you're a Venus flytrap.

Most plants are able to get the nutrients they need from the soil. But in some areas, the soil lacks an essential nutrient that plants need in order to survive. Certain plants have evolved an unusual adaptation to obtain the nutrient that is missing from the soil. They catch and digest insects. One carnivorous plant is the Venus flytrap, found mostly in North and South Carolina.

▶ Before You Read

BUGGED Many animals capture insects for food. Fill in the chart below to identify the method each animal uses to capture insects.

ANIMAL	HOW IT CATCHES INSECTS
spider	
frog	
bat	

▶ Read

NOTEZONE

This reading mentions the word "jaws" eight times. Underline the sentence that explains what the "jaws" actually are.

Some plants have more in common with carnivorous animals than you might expect.

A Mean, Green Predator

Snap! The two jaws slam shut on the clumsy animal. The long, thin teeth interlock, so that escape is impossible. The jaws press closer together, crushing the creature. Digestive juices flow, slowly breaking down its soft tissues. After the resulting broth has been absorbed...the jaws open and the remains of the prey are dropped.

Too bad for the victim. It shouldn't have been so careless around this hungry predator. And what predator is that? Alligator? Wolf? Snake? Shark? Squat little plant? It's a squat little plant—the Venus flytrap. Of course, they're not real jaws. They only look like jaws. And move like jaws. And capture like jaws. But the jaws are really just a leaf.

---

interlock: join together—like your fingers when your grip your hands together

digestive juices: chemicals that break down food

broth: a liquid in which meat or other foods are mixed

absorbed: taken in

prey: an organism that is eaten by another organism

predator: an organism that eats another organism

squat: low to the ground

From: Kneidel, Sally. *Skunk Cabbage, Sundew Plants & Strangler Figs: And 18 More Of The Strangest Plants On Earth.* John Wiley & Sons, Inc.

FIND OUT MORE

SCIENCESAURUS

Feeding
Relationships   133

Scientists have identified more than 500 species of carnivorous plants. Different species have different adaptations for attracting and capturing insects.

MAKE INFERENCES Use the following descriptions and pictures to infer how each plant attracts and traps insects.

Most species of pitcher plants are found in the southeastern United States. The plant's leaves are shaped like a pitcher. The outside of the pitcher is colorful and looks like a flower. The pitcher is lined with small, stiff hairs that point downward. At the bottom of the pitcher are digestive juices.

▶ *How do you think a pitcher plant attracts and captures insects?*

_____

_____

_____

_____

_____

Pitcher plant (Sarracenia rubra)

Sundew plants are found all over the world. Their leaves are covered with hundreds of hairs. At the tip of each hair is a drop of sticky fluid that shines like nectar in a flower. This fluid contains digestive juices. When a leaf is touched, it folds up like a fist.

▶ *How do you think a sundew attracts and captures insects?*

_____

_____

_____

_____

_____

Common Sundew (Drosera rotundifolia)

Butterwort plants are found mostly in North America, Asia, and Europe. The plant's leaves lie flat on the ground. The leaves are covered with a shiny, sticky liquid. The leaves curl up slowly when they are touched.

▶ *How do you think a butterwort attracts and captures insects?*

_____

_____

_____

_____

_____

_____

Butterwort
(Pinguicula moranensis)

CREATE A PLANT Design your own carnivorous plant. Draw and label a diagram to show how the plant attracts and traps insects.

Plant Adaptations

What Attracts Insects to Flowers?

Flowering plants and insects depend on each other to survive.

Flowering plants and insects have a mutualistic relationship. Flowers produce nectar that is food for insects. Insects carry pollen from flower to flower, which enables plants to reproduce. Flowers have adaptations that attract insects. These adaptations include the color of the petals, nectar, and honey guides. Honey guides are lines that lead to the flower's center, where the nectar and pollen are located.

▲ **Ladybug beetles (*Coleomegilla maculata*)**

▶ **Activity**

TESTING FLOWERS

Which feature—color, honey guides, or nectar—is most important for attracting insects? Put the question to the test by making model flowers.

What You Need:

- cardboard
- pink and white construction paper
- scissors
- thin black marker
- 8 skewers
- honey (small jar)

honey guide

What to Do:

1. Make a cardboard pattern for a flower shaped like the one shown here. The flower should be 6–8 cm wide.
2. Trace your pattern on construction paper to make four pink flowers and four white flowers. Cut out the flowers.
3. Number the pink flowers 1–4. Number the white flowers 5–8.
4. Use the black marker to draw honey guides on Flowers 1, 2, 5, and 6.
5. Stick a skewer through the center of each flower.

FIND OUT MORE

SCIENCESAURUS

Plant Life Cycles 108
Sexual
  Reproduction   114

UNIT 3: LIVING THINGS

Flower	Color	Honey Guides	Honey	Number of Insects
Flower 1	pink	yes	yes	
Flower 2	pink	yes	no	
Flower 3	pink	no	yes	
Flower 4	pink	no	no	
Flower 5	white	yes	yes	
Flower 6	white	yes	no	
Flower 7	white	no	yes	
Flower 8	white	no	no	

6. Choose a sunny day when flowers are blooming. Go outside and stick the model flowers in the ground. Put them close to each other.

7. Put a drop of honey in the center of Flowers 1, 3, 5, and 7.

▶ *Which flower do you think will attract the most insects? Why?*

_____

_____

▶ *Which flower do you think will attract the fewest insects? Why?*

_____

_____

8. Observe your model flowers for 15 minutes. Each time an insect lands on a flower, make a tally mark in the last column of the chart. After 15 minutes, count the tally marks in each box and write the number.

▶ *Which flower attracted the most insects?* _____

▶ *Compare the counts for Flowers 2–7. Which feature do you think is most important in attracting insects? What evidence do you have to support your choice?*

_____

_____

_____

_____

_____

_____

_____

UNIT 4 Human Body Systems

Do you know how strong your heart is?

End to end, your blood vessels could circle the globe more than twice! The heart needs to be strapping and tough in order to push blood that far. There are certain things you can do to keep it that way—like paying attention to what you eat, whether you smoke, and how much exercise you get.

Your body is like an all-star team— every part plays a specific role that contributes to the good of the whole. The body is a series of systems, each taking care of a few things in a very efficient way. In this unit, you'll learn about some of the most important systems. One system collects and distributes information, one helps you move around, and another processes the food you eat. Another system helps keep the health of your body in check, and like the coach or captain, your brain oversees it all. Working together, these systems make the body a winner!

THE CHAPTERS IN
THIS UNIT ARE . . .

CHAPTER 13:
Coming to Our Senses
Find Out: How do your ears help you keep your balance?

CHAPTER 14:
Body Work
Find Out: How many times does your heart beat each day?

CHAPTER 15:
A Mind of Its Own
Find Out: How does an optical illusion work?

CHAPTER 16:
Diseases Through Time
Find Out: What animal spreads malaria from one person to another?

? DID YOU KNOW

Sleep is as crucial to the human body as food and water. Starvation takes a few weeks without food, but death will occur after about only 10 days without sleep!

135

Coming to Our Senses

Testing Taste Buds

Thanks to your tongue, you can enjoy many flavors. Is fat one of them?

Your tongue is covered with tiny structures called taste buds. Sense cells inside the taste buds detect four basic tastes— sweet, sour, salty, and bitter. The flavors of most foods are a combination of these tastes plus the odors detected by your nose. But what about fat? Many people like fatty foods such as butter, cheese, and fried foods. Does fat have its own taste? To try to find an answer, scientist Richard Mattes did some "tasteful" research.

 **Before You Read**

FOOD FOR THOUGHT Imagine that you are visiting your local supermarket. As you wheel your shopping cart down the aisles, you fill it only with foods that have a high fat content, such as ice cream, butter, and potato chips.

▶ *List five other foods that you would include in your cart.*

_____

_____

_____

Many people today are concerned about eating a healthy diet. As a result, some food companies have produced "low-fat" or "fat-free" versions of their normally "fat-full" products.

▶ *Have you ever tried foods such as fat-free cream cheese or fat-free cookies? If so, describe what they tasted like.*

_____

_____

_____

_____

_____

▶ **Read**

Read about the experiment Dr. Richard Mattes conducted to find out whether fat has its own taste.

SURPRISE! FAT PROVES A TASTE SENSATION

For [many years], scientists...argued that fat has no taste...[because] our mouths lack taste buds...[that are] tuned to fat. That view may be slipping away.... By studying 19 adults, Richard D. Mattes of Purdue University in West Lafayette, Indiana, has shown that the [amount of eaten] fat that travels...into a person's bloodstream depends on whether the person tasted fat to begin with.

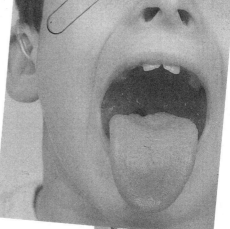

Mattes had volunteers come into his lab... after an overnight fast. [Some volunteers] ate a capsule of fat that they could neither smell nor taste. [Other volunteers] fasted for 8 more hours. [In some tests] the volunteers sniffed whiffs of cream cheese. [In other tests] they rolled cream cheese in their mouths...then spit it out. For [these tests, some] volunteers wore nose clips....

Mattes [measured the fat] in the volunteers' blood during each test. When the volunteers ate nothing, [fat levels] fell...whether [or not] they had tasted or smelled a fatty food. [When] participants [ate] a capsule of fat, [fat levels] rose.... When [participants ate a] fat capsule [then later] tasted cream cheese but didn't smell it, [the level of fat in the blood was three times greater than] when [they] only smelled the cheese....

fast: a period of time without eating any solid or liquid food
capsule: a small pill, usually with a gelatin covering, that contains a substance

participants: people who take part in an activity

From: Raloff, Janet. "Surprise! Fat Proves A Taste Sensation." *Science News.*

FIND OUT MORE

SCIENCESAURUS
The Five Senses   096

THE WORLD'S A CLICK AWAY

www.scilinks.org
Keyword: The Senses
Code: GSLD18

EXPERIMENT PROCEDURE The chart below summarizes all the tests in Dr. Mattes's experiment.

	TEST 1	TEST 2	TEST 3	TEST 4	TEST 5
Step1	fasted overnight, then came to lab	fasted overnight, then came to lab	fasted overnight, then came to lab	fasted overnight, then came to lab	fasted overnight, then came to lab
Step2	ate fat capsule	ate fat capsule	ate fat capsule	fasted for 8 more hours	fasted for 8 more hours
Step3	no nose clips; rolled cream cheese in mouth for 10 seconds, then spit it out	wore nose clips; rolled cream cheese in mouth for 10 seconds, then spit it out	sniffed whiffs of cream cheese for a couple of hours	no nose clips; rolled cream cheese in mouth for 10 seconds, then spit it out	did not smell or taste cream cheese

ANALYZE A GRAPH This graph shows the results of the experiment.

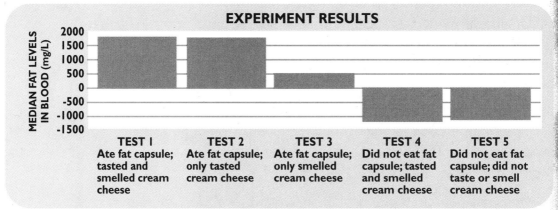

► *In which two tests were fat levels the highest? What variables were the same in both of those tests?*

_____

_____

► *Was it necessary to already have fat in the blood to get high fat levels in the tests?*

_____

_____

► *Which test was the control in the experiment?*

_____

Propose Explanations

WHAT DO YOU THINK?

▶ *Why did Dr. Mattes have the volunteers fast overnight?*

_____

_____

_____

▶ *Why did Dr. Mattes have the volunteers wear nose clips in Test 2?*

_____

_____

_____

▶ *If you were a scientist working with Dr. Mattes, what other questions about the sense of taste would you research?*

_____

_____

_____

▶ *Another scientist, Dr. Edmund T. Rolls, doesn't agree with Dr. Mattes's interpretation of the results. He thinks that fat levels in the blood may increase when the tongue senses the texture of fat (how it feels in the mouth), not its taste. What would you do to test Dr. Rolls's hypothesis?*

_____

_____

_____

_____

Take Action

DO RESEARCH How much of a jellybean's flavor is due to its appearance? Try this experiment. Write the numbers 1 through 5 on paper bags. Put 20 of one flavor of jellybean in each bag—a different flavor for each bag. Provide 10 cups of water. Ask 10 students to close their eyes, eat a jellybean from each bag, and write down what flavor they think it is. Between jellybeans, the students should take a few sips of water to rinse their mouths. Then have them repeat the experiment with their eyes open. Make a chart of your results. Did not seeing the jellybeans make it harder for the students to identify the flavors accurately?

Balancing Act

Your ears not only enable you to hear—they also help you keep your balance.

Learning to ride a bicycle takes skill, practice, and a sense of balance. To keep your balance, your brain has to receive information from many parts of your body. These include motion detectors in your inner ear, pressure detectors in your skin, stretch detectors in your muscles and skin, and visual clues from your eyes.

▶ Before You Read

THINK ABOUT IT Most of the time, you take your sense of balance for granted. Whether you're walking down the street or lifting a heavy object, you don't think about how your body keeps from falling over or tipping to one side.

But there are certain times when the human sense of balance seems remarkable. Think about the tight-rope walker at a circus. Imagine a child who has learned to ride a bicycle. Write down some of your favorite sports or other activities that require a strong sense of balance.

NOTEZONE

Underline all the things in your ear that help you keep your balance.

▶ Read

How do your ears help you stand up?

This Way Up

Sit up straight—you might learn something! It's as easy as falling off a log. How do you know? The little...hairs [inside your inner ear] tell you. Your ear is not just about hearing. It is also about balance. In your inner ear are three tubes, joined to each other at right angles. They are filled with fluid that sloshes about when you move your head. The [movements] of the fluid bend these hairs and tell your brain exactly where your head is.

---

right angle: a 90-degree angle, such as that in the corner of a square

sloshes: splashes back and forth inside a container

From: Janulewicz, Mike. *Yikes! Your Body, Up Close.* Simon & Schuster, Inc.

UNIT 4: HUMAN BODY SYSTEMS

FOOLING YOUR SENSE OF BALANCE

Find out what happens to the sense of balance when sensory information is not received from the eyes.

What You Need: firm cushion, blindfold (such as a handkerchief)

What to Do:

1. Ask a volunteer to stand on the cushion in stocking feet. Put the blindfold over the volunteer's eyes. *Caution:* Have another student stand near the volunteer to prevent him or her from falling.

2. Have the volunteer hold both arms out to the side and try to stand on one foot. Can the volunteer balance well? Record your observations.

3. Have the volunteer remove the blindfold, step off the cushion, and stand on the floor. Put the blindfold on the volunteer again. Have the volunteer repeat step 2. How was the volunteer's sense of balance affected by wearing the blindfold? Record your observations on the chart.

WHAT DID YOU SEE?

Standing on cushion	Standing on floor

WHAT DO YOU THINK?

▶ *Why do you think it was more difficult for the volunteer to balance on the cushion than on the bare floor?*

_____

_____

▶ *Why was it difficult for the volunteer to balance with the blindfold on?*

_____

_____

_____

▲ **Korean tightrope walker**

141

Coming to Our Senses

How Does It Feel?

You have knowledge about the sense of touch right at your fingertips.

What's the largest organ of the human body? The liver? The lungs? You might be surprised to learn that the answer is your skin. Your skin provides your brain with important information about the world around you through your sense of touch.

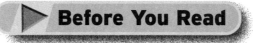

▶ Before You Read

MAKING SENSE Think about all the different kinds of information you get through your sense of touch. By running your finger over a surface, you can tell if it is rough or smooth, wet or dry. If you accidentally touch the blade of a very sharp knife, the skin on your fingers sends a pain message to your brain.

▶ *Describe an example of a time when your sense of touch helped you avoid being injured.*

_____

_____

_____

_____

Christmas beetles ▶

▶ Read

NOTEZONE

Underline the examples of the fine touch system.

Circle the example of the pain system.

A middle school student wrote to a website and asked how our nerves know the difference between something that hurts and something that tickles. Here's what a scientist had to say.

Hey, That Tickles! Ouch, Now THAT Hurts!

Question: How do our nerves distinguish between what hurts and what tickles?

Answer: We have two kinds of nerves for touch in our body. One kind is very good at detecting pain, while the other kind is good at detecting fine touch. For example, when you hold a fluffy towel, run a finger over sandpaper, or are tickled, you're using your fine-touch system. Your nerves send a message to your brain, and your brain interprets the signal as a soft touch.

Pain nerves are activated when something has happened that might be harmful to you. Hurtful things like a pinch, a burn, and hammering your thumb instead of the nail activate both your pain system and your fine-touch system. Nerves quickly send a signal to your spinal cord and then to your brain, and you feel pain.

system: a group of parts that carry out a function
activate: set into operation

From: *MadSci Network*. Washington University Medical School. (www.madsci.org)

FIND OUT MORE

SCIENCESAURUS
Nervous System   095
The Five Senses   096

143

Activity

GETTING IN TOUCH WITH TOUCH

You and a partner can test each other's touch systems.

What You Need:
- a partner
- metric ruler
- 5 paper clips (standard size)
- tape
- blindfold
- pen

What to Do:
1. Straighten a paper clip to make a skin tester with one point.
2. Bend a second paper clip into a U shape. Use a metric ruler to space the two points 0.5 cm apart. Wrap a small piece of tape around the U to keep the points from moving apart. Use a pen to label this piece of tape "0.5 cm."
3. Repeat step 2 to make and label paper clip U's with points that are 1 cm, 2 cm, and 3 cm apart.
4. Ask your partner to sit and put on a blindfold. Using one of the five paper clip testers, *gently* touch your partner's skin with both points of each tester in the five different places listed in the chart. Ask your partner to tell you how many points he or she feels. Record that number in the box that tells the points you used.
5. Repeat step 4 with each of the other four testers. Record the results.
6. Change places with your partner and repeat steps 4 and 5.

POINTS TOUCHED TO MY PARTNER'S SKIN					
TESTING AREAS	**One point**	**Two points**			
		0.5 cm apart	1 cm apart	2 cm apart	3 cm apart
Fingertip					
Palm of hand					
Back of hand					
Inside of lower arm					
Outside of lower arm					

144

▶ Propose Explanations

WHAT DID YOU LEARN?

▶ *Which skin area felt two points the most often? In other words, which skin area is most sensitive to touch?*

_____

▶ *Which skin area felt two points the least often? In other words, which skin area is least sensitive to touch?*

_____

▶ *Why did the test include using a paper clip with only one point?*

_____

▶ *What surprised you about the results of this test?*

_____

_____

The distance between sensory receptors on your skin is not the same all over your body. That's what makes the skin in some places more sensitive to touch than the skin in other places.

▶ *Based on your test, where do you think touch receptors are closest together?*

_____

▶ *Where do you think touch receptors are farthest apart?*

_____

▶ *Why do you think touch receptors are closer together in some areas than in others?*

_____

_____

▶ Take Action

MAKE A "TOUCH BOOK" Create a book that would help a young child explore the sense of touch. Attach objects with different textures to the pages, and add words that invite the child to touch the pages. For example, a page might have a piece of rough sandpaper, a piece of smooth plastic, something sticky, something soft, and so on. (*Caution:* Make sure all the objects are safe for a young child.) Give the book to a young child to enjoy.

Body Work

In One End...

After you finish your lunch, it continues on a journey through your digestive system.

How does your body break down the tasty food you eat to release the energy in it? How does your body separate the parts of the food you need from the parts you don't need? Both functions are performed by the digestive system. The organs that make up this system work together to break down food, absorb the substances you need, and get rid of the waste materials.

▶ **Before You Read**

CRUNCHING AND MUNCHING Digestion begins as soon as you put a piece of food in your mouth. Your teeth act like a food processor, chopping up food into smaller pieces. Saliva helps, too, by moistening the food to make it easier to swallow. Saliva contains chemicals called *enzymes* that start to break down food before you even swallow it.

Although you eat every day, you may have never thought about what's going on inside your mouth as you chew. To help you explore the first part of the digestive system, start by chewing a piece of carrot. As you chew, pay close attention to what is happening in your mouth.

▶ *How did your tongue help "process" the carrot?*

_____

_____

_____

_____

▶ *How did your teeth "process" the carrot?*

_____

_____

_____

_____

▶ Read

Number the three mechanical tasks of the stomach.

(Circle) the names of all the digestive organs mentioned in this reading.

Digestion begins in your mouth, but there's a lot more that has to happen to food before your body can use the nutrients in it. After you swallow food, what happens next?

Digesting Food Takes Guts

[When] food...enters the stomach, [it] has three mechanical tasks to do. First, the stomach must store the swallowed food and liquid. This requires the muscle of the upper part of the stomach to relax and accept large volumes of swallowed material. The second job is to mix up the food, liquid, and digestive juice produced by the stomach. The lower part of the stomach mixes these materials by its muscle action. The third task of the stomach is to empty its contents slowly into the small intestine.

As the food is digested in the small intestine and dissolved into the juices from the pancreas, liver, and intestine, the contents of the intestine are mixed and pushed forward to allow further digestion....The digested nutrients are absorbed through the [walls of the small intestine]. The waste products...are [pushed] into the [large intestine], where they remain, usually for a day or two, until the feces are expelled by a bowel movement.

nutrients: substances in food that the body needs in order to function properly
feces: the waste products of digestion

▲ X ray of large and small intestines

SCIENCESAURUS

Tissues, Organs, and Systems 082
Digestive System 089

SCILINKS
THE WORLD'S A CLICK AWAY

www.scilinks.org
Keyword:
Digestive System
Code: GSLD19

From: "Your Digestive System and How It Works." *National Digestive Diseases Information Clearinghouse.* National Institutes of Health. (www.niddk.nih.gov/health/digest/pubs/digesyst/newdiges.htm)

© GREAT SOURCE. COPYING IS PROHIBITED.

147

CREATE A MODEL

Make this model and use it to "digest" some food. Compare the model to what you know about how your own stomach works.

What You Need:
- gallon-sized plastic resealable bag
- soft, ripe banana, peeled and sliced
- 3 crushed crackers
- 3 tablespoons of water
- 3 or 4 drops of food coloring (red, blue, or green)

What to Do:
1. Put the banana, crushed crackers, water, and food coloring into the bag.
2. Flatten the bag to get most of the air out. Then seal the bag tightly.

▶ *What do you observe happening inside the bag?*

_____

_____

_____

3. Gently mash and squeeze the bag for 15–30 seconds. Examine the contents again.

▶ *What do the contents look like now?*

_____

_____

_____

_____

INTERPRET YOUR MODEL

▶ *In your model, what did your hands represent?*

_____

_____

▶ *What did the water and food coloring represent?*

_____

_____

▶ Propose Explanations

DRAW CONCLUSIONS

▶ *How do the churning motions of the stomach muscles help with digestion?*

_____

_____

_____

▶ *If food were not broken into smaller pieces in the mouth, what do you think would happen in the stomach?*

_____

_____

_____

▶ *How could you improve this model so that it more accurately shows all three mechanical tasks of the stomach?*

_____

_____

_____

▶ *In the small intestine, the partly digested food is mixed with digestive juices from the liver and pancreas. What structures do you think produce this mixing action?*

_____

_____

_____

▶ Take Action

IT SLICES, IT DICES, IT DIGESTS On a separate sheet of paper, design your own model that performs all the functions of the digestive system you've learned about. Make sure your model includes each part of the digestive system. Draw a diagram of your model. Add arrows to your diagram to show the passage of food through the model. Label the diagram to tell what each part of the model does.

Body Work

The Beat Goes On

That thump-THUMP, thump-THUMP in your chest is the sound of your heart sending blood throughout your body.

Most of the time, you probably take your heart for granted. You don't think about the number of times that this powerful organ beats each day, sending oxygen-rich blood throughout your body. Since every cell in your body needs oxygen, your heart has a very important role.

 ▶ **Before You Read**

BY HEART Draw the heart in this picture of a person's chest. Show what you think is the heart's shape and size and its location in the chest.

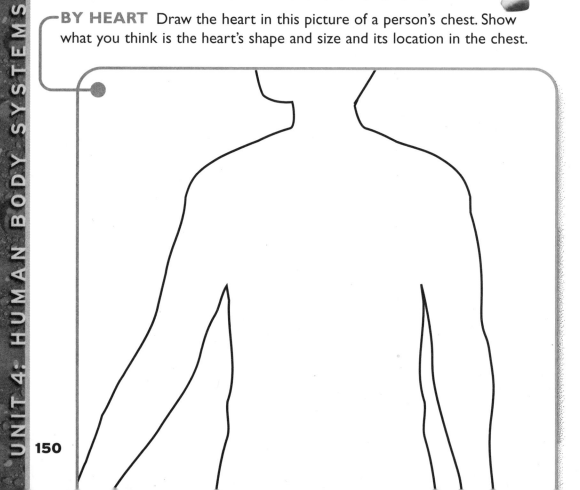

UNIT 4: HUMAN BODY SYSTEMS

▶ Read

You know your heart pumps blood, but there's a lot more to this incredible organ.

AMAZING HEART FACTS

- In one day, your blood travels a total of 19,000 km (12,000 miles)—that's four times the distance across the U.S. from coast to coast.

- Your heart beats about 100,000 times in one day and about 35 million times in a year....

- Put your hand on your heart. Did you place your hand on the left side of your chest? Many people do, but the heart is actually located almost in the center of the chest, between the lungs. It's tipped slightly so that a part of it sticks out and taps against the left side of the chest, which is what makes it seem as though it is located there.

- If you're a kid, your heart is about the same size as your fist, and if you're an adult, it's about the same size as two fists.

- Give a tennis ball a good, hard squeeze. You're using about the same amount of force your heart uses to pump blood out to the body....

From: "Amazing Heart Facts." *Nova Online*. WGBH. (www.pbs.org/wgbh/nova/heart/heartfacts.html)

▶ **Heart of an adult woman**

NOTEZONE

About how many times does your heart beat during one science class?

▶ Explore

UNHEALTHY HEARTS Hundreds of thousands of Americans lose their lives each year to heart attacks, strokes, and other heart-related diseases. But back in 1900, only about 25,000 people in the U.S. died of heart disease. That's about 33 deaths per 100,000 people. Compare that with about 266 deaths per 100,000 people in 1999. What caused this dramatic increase in heart-related deaths? One reason may be that people in 1999 were living longer than people did in 1900, so they were more likely to experience heart disease, which occurs more frequently with age. Scientists are investigating other causes as well.

FIND OUT MORE

SCIENCESAURUS
Circulatory System 093

151

ANALYZE A GRAPH Use the graph to answer the following questions.

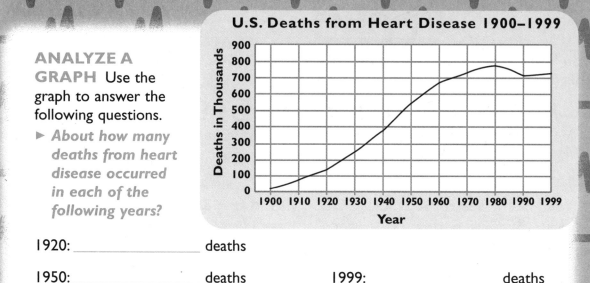

U.S. Deaths from Heart Disease 1900–1999

▶ *About how many deaths from heart disease occurred in each of the following years?*

1920: _____ deaths

1950: _____ deaths   1999: _____ deaths

▶ *When were heart-related deaths most common?*

_____

▶ *Since 1980, what has happened to the number of deaths from heart disease?*

_____

_____

EXAMINE THE RISK FACTORS Not everyone has the same risk of developing heart disease. According to doctors, people who are likely to develop heart disease share a number of risk factors—conditions and behaviors that may lead to the disease. People cannot control some risk factors, such as their age, but there are other factors that people can control.

RISK FACTORS THAT CAN BE CONTROLLED

SMOKING Smoking increases the risk of heart disease.

HIGH CHOLESTEROL People with high amounts of fatty cholesterol in their blood are more than twice as likely to develop heart disease. Fatty cholesterol is found in high-fat foods such as ice cream, butter, and fried foods.

HIGH BLOOD PRESSURE One in four American adults has high blood pressure. Eating salty foods, drinking alcohol, smoking, not getting enough exercise, and being overweight can all contribute to high blood pressure.

LACK OF EXERCISE Lack of exercise contributes to more than 25,000 deaths from heart disease a year.

OBESITY People who are extremely overweight are three times more likely to develop heart disease.

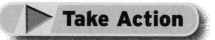

▶ Propose Explanations

PUTTING IT TOGETHER Think about how the daily activities and habits of Americans have changed over the last 100 years.

▶ *In 1900, there was no such thing as "convenience foods." Most people had to cook their own food or buy it from someone else who cooked it. How is this different from the situation today?*

_____

_____

▶ *How has this diet change affected the number of people who develop heart disease?*

_____

_____

_____

▶ *Think about the kinds of work that most Americans did in the early 1900s and the kinds of work Americans do now. Do Americans today get more or less daily exercise than they did then? What are some inventions that have contributed to this change?*

_____

_____

_____

▶ *Look back at the list of risk factors that can be controlled. In order for the number of annual heart-related deaths in the U.S. to decrease, how would Americans need to change their lifestyles?*

_____

_____

▶ Take Action

DEVELOP A PLAN Most types of heart disease take years to develop. The health habits you develop as a teenager could affect your risk of developing heart disease when you're older. On a separate sheet of paper, create a healthy menu and exercise plan for one week. Explain how each of the foods and behaviors in your plan could affect your risk factors for heart disease. Find out about other benefits of these health habits.

Body Work

On the Move

Jumping, kicking, and even breathing would be impossible without your mighty muscles.

Sometimes in a movie, the good guy will tell the bad guy, "Don't move a muscle." In real life, it's impossible for a living person to stop all muscle activity. Just standing still takes constant muscle activity. Also, many muscles in your body are constantly in motion, such as those in your digestive system and your heart. Other muscles you can control.

NOTEZONE

Which kind of muscles are used when you do jumping jacks?

▶ **Read**

There are three types of muscles in your body.

Muscles and Motion

Muscles are the motors of the human body, allowing us to walk, pumping our blood, making us breathe and pushing our food through the digestive system. In order to do these different types of jobs, muscles come in three forms. Cardiac muscle is found only in the heart, smooth muscle lines our blood vessels and digestive system, and skeletal muscle makes us move.

...[Skeletal] muscle is...made up of thousands of individual cells, each wrapped in connective tissue. These elongated cells, referred to as fibers, are arranged in bundles. Thin threadlike structures called myofibrils run through each fiber, and when a muscle contracts, these myofibrils pull past each other, shortening the cells.

Skeletal muscles create motion by pulling on tough cords of connective tissue called tendons. These tendons in turn pull on the bone, which creates motion. Since muscles can only contract, each joint must have two opposing sets of muscles to give the full range of motion.

▼ **Cardiac muscle tissue**

FIND OUT MORE

SCIENCESAURUS

Muscular System 087

cardiac: having to do with the heart

vessels: thin tubes in the body that carry blood

skeletal: attached to or formed by the skeleton

elongated: long and thin

contracts: tightens and shortens

From: "Muscles and Bones; Einstein; Stars Chat; Raptor Center." *Newton's Apple.* KTCA. (www.pbs.org/ktca/newtons/newtonsclassics/classic11.html)

▶ Explore

GOING UP, GOING DOWN Hold a heavy book in one hand, and put your other hand around your upper arm. Lift the book up toward your shoulder very slowly. What do you feel in your upper arm? Now slowly lower the book. What do you feel in your upper arm?

_____

_____

_____

▶ *Which type of muscle did you use?* _____

▶ Propose Explanations

THINK ABOUT IT The muscle at the front of your upper arm is called the biceps. The muscle at the back of your upper arm is called the triceps.

▶ *Explain what your biceps and triceps did as you raised and lowered the book. How could you tell what the muscles were doing? (Hint: Remember what you learned in the reading about skeletal muscles working in pairs.)*

_____

_____

_____

_____

_____

_____

▶ *As you lowered the book, did the biceps relax completely? Why do you think that happened?*

_____

_____

_____

_____

_____

A Mind of Its Own

Brain Scan

The human brain is an amazing organ. It's even beginning to figure itself out!

Your brain runs the show. It creates what you think, what you feel, and what you do. One of the ways your brain does this is by using different areas for different things. But these different areas are constantly communicating with each other.

▶ **Read**

NOTEZONE

What other questions do you have after reading this?

Here is one description of the brain.

DON'T BE FOOLED

The brain is the body's control center. It is involved with what we do and what we think as well as what we feel and remember. We also use our brains to learn. [Generally,] the left-hand side of our brain controls the right side of the body, and the right-hand side of our brain controls the left side of the body.

It has been found that each side of our brain is responsible for different skills. The right side holds our artistic talent and imagination, and the left side is more responsible for practical abilities and logical thinking.

practical: having to do with ordinary activities
logical: having to do with reasoning

From: Barnes, Kate, and Steve Weston. *How it Works: The Human Body.* Barnes & Noble Books

FIND OUT MORE

SCIENCESAURUS
Nervous System   095

SCI LINKS.
THE WORLD'S A CLICK AWAY
www.scilinks.org
Keyword: Human Brain
Code: GSLD20

UNIT 4: HUMAN BODY SYSTEMS

156

Explore

THINKING ABOUT THINKING A brain scan is a picture of the brain. One kind of brain scan shows the areas we are using lit up. Scientists use brain scans to show which areas of the brain are active during an activity. For example, the diagrams below show which areas of your brain are active when you use language.

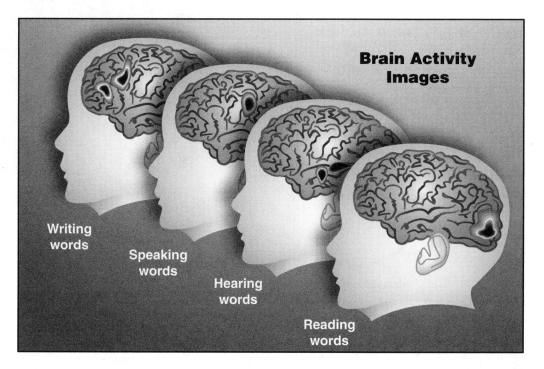

Brain Activity Images

Writing words

Speaking words

Hearing words

Reading words

▶ *Study the diagrams. Is your entire brain active when you use language?*

_____

_____

▶ *During a stroke, some areas of the brain can be injured. What problems could a person have after a stroke if the areas shown in the diagrams were injured?*

_____

_____

_____

_____

_____

A Mind of Its Own

SLEEP ON IT

You've probably heard that it's important to get a good night's sleep. There may now be scientific evidence to back that up.

It's 11 P.M. and you have a big math test tomorrow morning. You've been studying for several hours and feel tired. But you'd like to go over a few more problems to make sure you understand how to solve them. Should you study some more or go to bed?

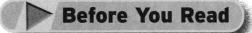

▶ Before You Read

SEQUENCE Think about the last time you had to study for a big test. What did you do the night before to prepare for it? Did you study continuously for a long time or in several short sessions? Did you study until the wee hours of the morning, or did you get up early the next morning to study? Describe what you did to prepare for the test.

_____

_____

_____

_____

_____

_____

_____

_____

_____

▶ Read

NOTE ZONE

Why do we sleep? No one really knows for sure. Some experiments, such as the one described below, suggest that sleep is important for learning.

Why Do We Sleep?

Human subjects were trained to identify letters that appeared for a blink of an eye on a computer screen. Then, half of the subjects were sent home to sleep, while the other half were deprived of sleep for the entire night.... Two days later...the scientists checked [the subjects'] ability to read the flashing letters. None of the [subjects] were tired and yet the people who went to sleep right after the training performed much better than the ones who went to sleep a day later. This suggests that the night sleep immediately after the activity was [very important] for gaining the most from the training session....

The fact that during...childhood and adolescence, people sleep much more than during their adulthood, also supports the view that sleeping plays a role in learning. Yet, some scientists claim that this evidence is still weak, and more importantly, that other experiments yield [opposite] results. Therefore, they argue, declaring that the mystery of sleep is resolved, and that the main function of sleep is to [help] learning, would be premature. Only future research can decide this debate.

subjects: the people who are studied in an experiment
deprived of: kept from
adolescence: the teenage years
premature: too early

From: "The Teenage Brain: Why Do We Sleep?,"
The Secret Life of the Brain

Circle and label the procedure, results, and conclusion in the experiment.

What variable was different between the two groups in the experiment?

FIND OUT MORE
SCIENCESAURUS
Nervous System 095

SLEEP STAGES A person's brain activity during sleep can be measured by a process called electroencephalography (EEG). Special sensors are attached to the skin on the person's skull. The sensors measure electrical activity in different parts of the brain. This shows which parts of the brain are active.

EEG tests show that people go through two main types of sleep during the night—slow wave sleep (SWS) and rapid eye movement (REM) sleep. Slow wave sleep can be divided into four separate stages according to the strength and frequency of the electrical activity in the brain. But none of the four stages is as active as rapid eye movement sleep. REM sleep is when we dream.

Sleep Stage	Characteristics of Stage
Slow wave sleep (SWS) (Stages 1–4)	Slow EEG activity
Rapid eye movement (REM) sleep	Very active EEG activity; dreaming

Look at the following graph. It shows the different stages of sleep that a person goes through in a typical night. The graph's vertical axis shows which stage of sleep the person is in. The horizontal axis shows how long the person has been sleeping. Use the graph to answer the questions below.

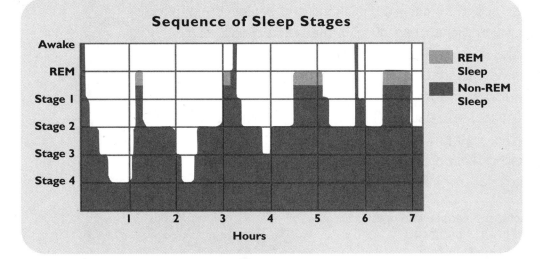

▶ *What happens to the length of each REM stage as the night goes on?*

_____

▶ *What pattern do you notice in the graph?*

_____

160

▶ Propose Explanations

THINK ABOUT IT Experiments suggest that during REM sleep, your brain reviews, sorts, and organizes the information that it has been exposed to during the day. Some of the information is stored and some is discarded.

▶ *Your friend says she'll do well on a test because she slept for three hours after studying late into the night. Based on the information in the graph and in the reading, how would you respond to your friend?*

_____

_____

_____

▶ *Why do scientists think that sleep, especially REM sleep, is important for learning?*

_____

_____

_____

▶ Take Action

SLEEP AND LEARN Test how sleep affects your memory. In the morning, study list A for 10 minutes. Then don't look at the list for the rest of the day. After eight hours have passed, write down all the words you can remember.

At night, right before going to bed, study list B for 10 minutes. Be sure to get about eight hours of sleep. Then in the morning, without looking at the list, write down as many words as you can remember.

▶ *How did sleep affect your ability to remember a list of words? Were you able to remember more words from list B? Write your results below. Share them with the class.*

List A	List B
horseshoe	quantity
category	medicine
sphinx	funnel
civilian	target
opinion	latitude
animate	scavenger
utility	ornament
segment	graceful
independent	stadium
magnify	journalist

A Mind of Its Own

Seeing Things

Your brain wouldn't play tricks on you, would it?

The brain may be a remarkable organ, but even *it* can be fooled. How does your brain get confused? One way is when it sees something different from what's really there. This is called an optical illusion.

▶ **Before You Read**

DON'T BE FOOLED! Look at this drawing.

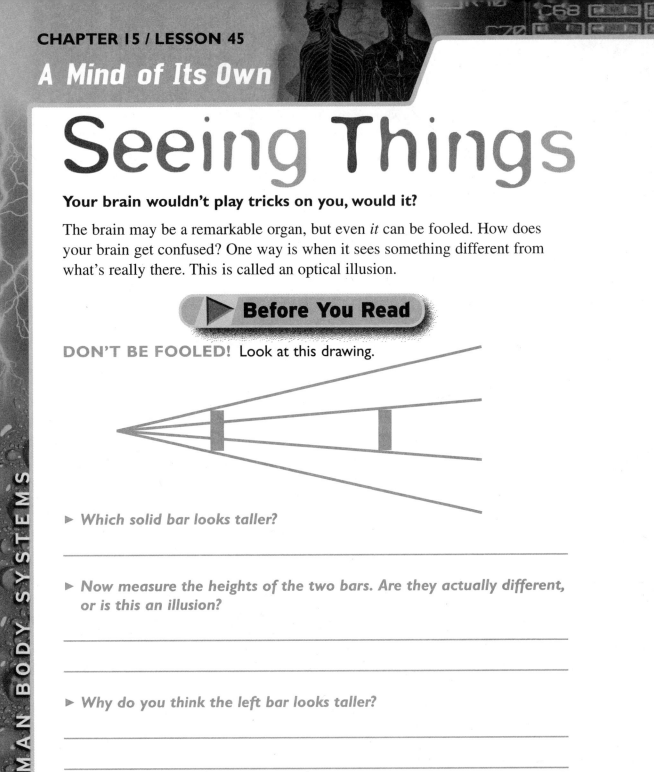

▶ *Which solid bar looks taller?*

_____

▶ *Now measure the heights of the two bars. Are they actually different, or is this an illusion?*

_____

_____

▶ *Why do you think the left bar looks taller?*

_____

_____

_____

_____

Read

NOTEZONE

Why does
the reading
say that
optical
illusions trick
the brain, not
the eye?

**How can your brain be fooled?
Here's how.**

Fooling the Brain

Optical illusions…are supposed to trick the eye.
But…[it's] the brain that is tricked. In early life,…we
learn many assumptions and shortcuts to help
understand what we see. For instance, if the brain is
presented with a regular pattern that has a piece
blocked out, it "assumes" the pattern continues into the
blank portion, since in daily life this is usually the case.
Many optical illusions play on these assumptions by
presenting images that do not normally occur in real life.
Others exploit the brain's attempts always to make
sense of the messages it gets from the eyes.

assumption: belief about what's true based on
what's been true before
exploit: make use of or take advantage of

From: Whitfield, Philip, ed. *The Human Body Explained: A Guide to Understanding
the Incredible Living Machine.* Henry Holt Co.

FIND OUT MORE

SCIENCESAURUS

Nervous System   095
The Five Senses   096

SEEING ISN'T BELIEVING Look at these optical illusions.

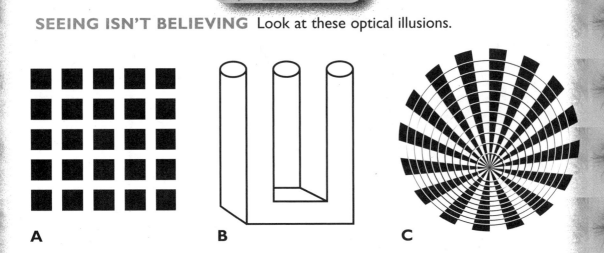

A   B   C

▶ *Describe what you see at first in each illusion. Then describe what you know is true after examining the illusion carefully.*

Illusion	What I see at first	Figure it out	What I know is true
A		Look at the point where the white lines cross. Then, cover up the squares around it.	
B		Trace your finger along the lines to see the entire shape.	
C		Trace your finger along the thin lines. What shape are they?	

▶ Take Action

BE A BRAIN TEASER Choose one of the optical illusions on page 164. Think about the assumption your brain makes that causes you to see the illusion. Then use that assumption to create your own optical illusion. For example, in the Before You Read illusion, the brain assumes that the bars are two different sizes. The slanted lines that hit the bars at different places trick the brain into thinking the bars are different sizes.

▶ *Make a drawing of your optical illusion.*

▶ *Describe the illusion you are trying to create.*

_____

_____

_____

_____

_____

▶ *Show your drawing to your classmates and find out what they see. Was your illusion successful? Why or why not?*

_____

_____

_____

_____

Diseases Through TIme

Conquering Polio

Until the mid-1900s, summer was a scary time. Parents were afraid that their children would get polio from public places like swimming pools and drinking fountains, and become handicapped or die.

Polio is a serious disease that attacks the nerves that control muscles. It is especially dangerous if it affects the muscles that enable a person to breathe or swallow. In the 1940s and '50s, thousands of children in the United States died each year from polio. Scientists worked hard to find a way to prevent the disease. Dr. Jonas Salk made the first polio vaccine from killed viruses. Dr. Albert Sabin made a vaccine from weakened live viruses. Thanks to these scientists, polio is no longer a major threat in this country.

▲ **Polio virus**

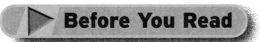 ▶ **Before You Read**

UNDER ATTACK When any disease-causing bacteria or virus enters your bloodstream, your body responds. Your immune system produces special proteins called antibodies—a different one for each type of germ. The antibodies attack the germs to try to prevent them from infecting the body's cells. The antibodies stay in the body for a period of time, even after the germs are gone. If the same kind of germ enters again, the antibodies are already there to attack the germ instantly. If a germ is very strong and attacks quickly, the body may not be able to respond in time to prevent a serious infection.

Vaccines made from viruses also cause the body to produce antibodies. But because the viruses are weakened or killed, they do not cause the actual disease.

THINK ABOUT IT

▶ *Why do you think injecting the body with a vaccine would help the body protect itself if it were to get the virus in the future?*

_____

_____

_____

UNIT 4: HUMAN BODY SYSTEMS

> **Read**

Dr. Jonas Salk wanted to make a vaccine against polio by using killed polio viruses.

JONAS EDWARD SALK

Salk...had developed a killed-virus vaccine.... Salk found that...the dead virus vaccine could cause the body to make...antibodies against polio. He had tested his vaccine on animals and had enough faith in it to inject it into himself, his family, and some friends.... In 1952 Salk conducted small but successful trials.... In all instances the antibody levels against the virus were [much higher]....

The [large-scale] field trial was started on April 26, 1954. Because parents were anxious for their children to have protection against polio...over 650,000 children in forty-four states received...injections of Salk vaccine.

The result, screamed in headlines all over the world: The vaccine was safe and it worked! [O]verall, it was between 80 and 90 percent effective against...polio.

Over the next several years there was a [big] decline in the number of polio cases.... [I]n 1952 a severe epidemic had caused 58,000 new cases of polio, [but] the number of cases reported in 1962 had dropped to just over 900. Polio was on its way out.

instances: reported cases
field trial: a test of a new product on the general public
epidemic: an outbreak of a disease that affects many people

From: Curtis, Robert H., M.D. *Medicine: Great Lives.* Charles Scribner's Sons Reference, a unit of Macmillan Library Reference USA.

Dr. Jonas Salk ▶

NoteZone

Make a bar graph to compare the number of new polio cases in 1952 and 1962.

FIND OUT MORE

SCIENCESAURUS
Immune System   098

SCILINKS
THE WORLD'S A CLICK AWAY
www.scilinks.org
Keyword: Vaccines
Code: GSLD21

DRAW A DIAGRAM Show what happens in the body as a result of vaccination. First, draw the body's response to the vaccine. Include the vaccine and the antibodies. Then draw what happens later when the person is infected by the live virus. Include the virus and the antibodies. Label your drawings.

▶ *Dr. Salk tested his polio vaccine on his family and friends. Do you think it was right to do that? Explain your answer.*

Propose Explanations

MAKE A PREDICTION
▶ *How would the body's response to a disease-causing virus be different without a vaccination?*

_____

_____

_____

_____

_____

Take Action

LIVING HISTORY Interview a family member or friend who was a child in the 1940s or 1950s. Ask the person to describe his or her memories of polio epidemics and of polio vaccinations. Take notes during the interview. Then write a brief account of the person's experiences.

_____

_____

_____

_____

_____

_____

_____

_____

_____

_____

Diseases Through TIme

THE BUZZ ON MALARIA

The word *malaria* means "bad air." People used to think that this disease was caused by breathing the air in swamps.

Malaria is an infectious disease spread by the *Anopheles* mosquito. In the mid-1900s, poisons were used to kill these mosquitoes, and malaria was nearly wiped out. Then the *Anopheles* species began to change as it became resistant to the poisons. In time, the poisons no longer worked. The number of malaria cases increased. If malaria is treated immediately, it can be cured. But the medicines are expensive and many people cannot afford them.

NOTEZONE

About how many children died of malaria during the time it took you to read this?

▶ **Read**

Time how long it takes you to read the following paragraphs.

Epidemic!

[M]alaria is…caused by one of several protozoan species of the genus *Plasmodium*. *Plasmodium* is spread to humans by the bite of the female *Anopheles* mosquito, which breeds in slow-moving, clear water.

The symptoms of malaria are fever and shaking chills, headache, and joint pain. During part of its life cycle, *Plasmodium* invades the red blood cells, using them as a place to reproduce and destroying the cells in the process. The result is severe anemia, and, often, fatal damage to the brain and other vital organs.

An estimated 300 million people are infected with malaria, and between 1 and 1.5 million die every year. Most of the victims are children, who die…before they are able to develop immunity. According to [the World Health Organization], a child dies of malaria every thirty seconds.

FIND OUT MORE

SCIENCESAURUS
Circulatory
  System   093
Immune System   098
Protist Kingdom   156

protozoan: a single-celled organism in the Protist kingdom
symptoms: signs of a disease
anemia: a condition of weakness caused by defective or not enough red blood cells

fatal: deadly
vital organs: body parts you need to survive
immunity: protection against a disease

From: DeSalle, Rob. *Epidemic!: The World of Infectious Disease*. The New Press

UNIT 4: HUMAN BODY SYSTEMS

170

Explore

FOLLOWING THE CHAIN

Plasmodium has a complex life cycle. It reproduces inside *Anopheles* mosquitoes. It is passed from one person to another by these mosquitoes. A mosquito bites a person who has malaria and sucks up the person's blood, which has the *Plasmodium* in it. When the same mosquito bites another person, some of the *Plasmodium* passes into that person's blood. That person may then become infected with malaria.

As long as *Anopheles* mosquitoes exist, malaria will continue to be passed along in an unbroken chain. The diagram shows the connection between people, *Anopheles,* and *Plasmodium*.

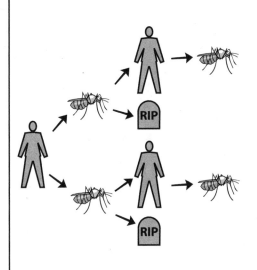

INTERPRETING THE DIAGRAM

▶ *What does each tombstone represent?*

_____

_____

▶ *According to the diagram, can malaria pass directly from one person to another person? Explain.*

_____

_____

▶ *Which organism involved in the spread of malaria cannot be seen in the diagram? Why not?*

_____

_____

_____

_____

▶ *Some people don't get malaria even if they're bitten by an infected* Anopheles *mosquito. Change the diagram above to include those people.*

◀ **Anopheles mosquito**

Diseases Through Time

HELP YOURSELF STAY HEALTHY

Children and adults get sick all the time. Here are some ways to help yourself stay healthy.

Infectious diseases are caused by many kinds of microscopic germs such as viruses, bacteria, and fungi. These germs can be passed from one person to another by coughing or sneezing, or when saliva or mucus gets on the infected person's hands and the person touches objects that are then touched by uninfected people. Germs cause illnesses that range from the common cold to more serious and sometimes deadly diseases such as polio, the flu, and pneumonia. The Centers for Disease Control and Prevention, a government agency, works to help reduce the spread of infectious diseases.

 ▶ **Before You Read**

THINK ABOUT IT What things do you do to keep from getting an infectious disease such as a cold?

_____

_____

_____

_____

_____

▶ *Think about the last time you had a cold, the flu, or another infectious disease. Do you know how you came into contact with the germs? Do you think you passed the germs on to someone else? What could you have done to better protect yourself from getting sick?*

_____

_____

_____

_____

UNIT 4: HUMAN BODY SYSTEMS

NOTEZONE

Which of these steps do you usually follow?

The Centers for Disease Control and Prevention suggests seven steps for helping to prevent infectious diseases.

AN OUNCE OF PREVENTION KEEPS THE GERMS AWAY

1. Wash your hands often. The proper way to wash your hands is to wet them first, apply soap, then rub and scrub them vigorously for 10 to 15 seconds. Rinse and dry.

2. Get immunized. Getting immunizations is easy, inexpensive, and saves lives.

3. Routinely clean and disinfect surfaces. Cleaning with soap, water, and scrubbing removes dirt and most germs. Disinfecting with a bleach solution or another disinfectant kills additional germs.

4. Use antibiotics appropriately. Antibiotics are powerful drugs used to treat certain bacterial infections. Antibiotics should be taken exactly as prescribed by your health care provider.

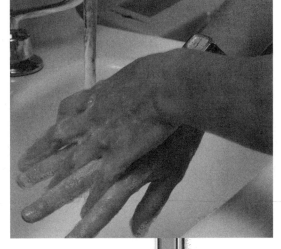

5. Handle and prepare food safely. Don't leave perishable food out for more than 2 hours. Wash your hands and clean and disinfect all kitchen surfaces and utensils before, during, and after handling, cooking, and serving food.

6. Keep pets healthy. Follow the schedule of immunizations. Obey local leash laws. Clean litter boxes daily.

7. Avoid contact with wild animals. Wild animals can carry diseases.

immunization: vaccination against disease
perishable food: food that will spoil or decay

From: "Facts About Infectious Diseases." *Centers for Disease Control and Prevention.* United States Department of Health and Human Services.

(www.cdc.gov/ncidod/op/materials/opbrochure.PDF)

FIND OUT MORE

SCIENCESAURUS

Immune System	098
Fungi Kingdom	155
Protist Kingdom	156
Kingdom Monera	157

Explore

KEEP IT CLEAN Many infectious bacteria live in raw or undercooked foods, so keeping the kitchen clean is very important. You should wash your hands before and after preparing food. You should even wash them during preparation—for example, after cutting meat and before making a salad. Counters and other surfaces should be cleaned and disinfected regularly. Paper towels are good to use for this because they can be thrown away. Cloth towels should be washed with detergent in very hot water.

Meat, poultry, seafood, and eggs are especially likely to carry infectious bacteria. These foods should be kept in separate containers so they won't contaminate other foods. Eggs should never be eaten raw or partially cooked. All poultry and meat should be cooked until the juices run clear. Cold foods should be kept cold, and hot foods should be kept hot.

USE WHAT YOU KNOW Suppose you are planning a picnic with your friends. At your picnic you plan to grill hamburgers. You want to have them with all the fixings—buns, ketchup, relish, lettuce, onion, tomato, and cheese. You also plan to take canned drinks and fresh fruit for dessert.

▶ *What steps should you take to make sure that your meal is as safe as possible from germs?*

_____

_____

_____

_____

_____

_____

_____

_____

_____

_____

_____

_____

_____

_____

MAKE OBSERVATIONS You and your classmates can help prevent the spread of infectious diseases in your school. Look around the school. Watch the activities that go on. Pay attention to what you and your classmates do. Do you see ways to use the seven steps to prevent infectious diseases? List them below.

_____

_____

_____

_____

MAKE A POSTER Design a poster to remind other students to do their part to keep your school healthy. Use the ideas in the list you made above. Draw cartoons to make your messages fun to read. Sketch your poster design in the space below.

UNIT 5 Ecology

Do you know what the word ecology means?

The *eco-* part comes from the Greek word *oikos*, which means "house." You probably already know that *-logy* at the end of a word means "study of." Put the two parts together and you have ecology, "the study of the house." But what is "the house"? Our home, of course—planet Earth.

In this unit you'll learn how different kinds of organisms interact with each other. Some of those interactions involve feeding relationships—coyotes eating rodents, for example. Other interactions involve different kinds of animals competing with each other for food and other resources. And in other interactions, two kinds of organisms interact in ways that benefit each other. You'll also explore how humans changed the environment in the past and how we're still changing it today.

THE CHAPTERS IN THIS UNIT ARE . . .

CHAPTER 17:
Populations, Communities, and Ecosystems

Find out: Why did farmers in Australia release cane toads into their fields?

CHAPTER 18:
Under the Grassland Sky

Find out: Do coyotes just eat meat, or do they eat plants and plant products, too?

CHAPTER 19:
Rain Forests

Find out: How is a tapir's upper lip like an elephant's trunk?

CHAPTER 20:
Protecting Earth

Find out: How many people are alive on Earth today?

? DID YOU KNOW

An adult coyote eats about 200 pounds (90 kilograms) of meat each year. That's equal to 75 jackrabbits or 100 cottontail rabbits or 5,000 ground squirrels!

Populations, Communities, and Ecosystems

The CANE TOAD Invasion

Populations of cane toads are flourishing in parts of Australia, and no one knows how to stop them!

Cane toads are normally found only in parts of South, Central, and North America. But in 1935 farmers in Gordonvale, Australia, sent for some of the toads, hoping they would eat the cane beetles that fed on sugar cane plants and damaged the crops. As it turned out, the toads were too big and clumsy to leap up and reach the beetles on the tall sugar cane stalks. The toads were good at something, though—making more toads.

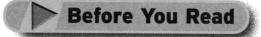 **Before You Read**

IDENTIFY POPULATIONS A population is a group of organisms of the same species that live in the same area. The cane toads released into the sugar fields of Gordonvale, Australia, formed one population. Soon the cane toad population grew and expanded into different areas to form new populations.

► *Name some populations you can identify in the area where you live. Explain why these groups are populations. Remember—plants, fungi, and microorganisms form populations, too.*

_____

_____

_____

_____

_____

_____

_____

▶ Read

NOTE ZONE

Circle the items in the list that describe how the toads interact with other living things in their environment.

Underline the items that describe how the toads interact with nonliving things in their environment.

When 102 cane toads were let loose in Gordonvale, Australia, the toad population began to grow at an alarming rate.

The Unwanted Amphibian

After arriving in Australia, the toads were on their own and they proved to be very hardy survivors. It didn't take long to find out how well the toads would do in their new home. There are many reasons why cane toads became a pest so quickly.

- They breed like flies, as the saying goes. Each pair can lay more than 30,000 eggs every few weeks during summer!

- Their young develop faster than many Australian frogs so they eat up much of the food before frogs can get to it.

- Toads seem to be resistant to some herbicides and poor quality water which would normally make frogs ill and die.

- Almost all stages of a toad's life are poisonous so they have no natural predators to keep their numbers in check.

- Toads not only eat the food normally available to Australian frogs, they also eat small frogs [and] other wildlife such as baby snakes.

hardy: capable of surviving in harsh conditions
breed: reproduce, make more of one's own kind
resistant: unaffected by
herbicides: chemicals used to kill unwanted plants
predators: organisms that hunt other organisms for food

From: "The Unwanted Amphibian." *Frog Decline Reversal Project.* Frog Decline Reversal Project, Inc. (www.fdrproject.org/pages/TDprogress.htm)

FIND OUT MORE

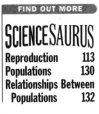

SCIENCESAURUS
Reproduction   113
Populations   130
Relationships Between
  Populations   132

WHERE DO CANE TOADS LIVE? Cane toads are native to parts of South, Central, and North America. Populations have also increased in places where the toads have been introduced by people, including Hawaii, Australia, the Philippines, Florida, and Puerto Rico. The following map shows the locations of cane toad populations.

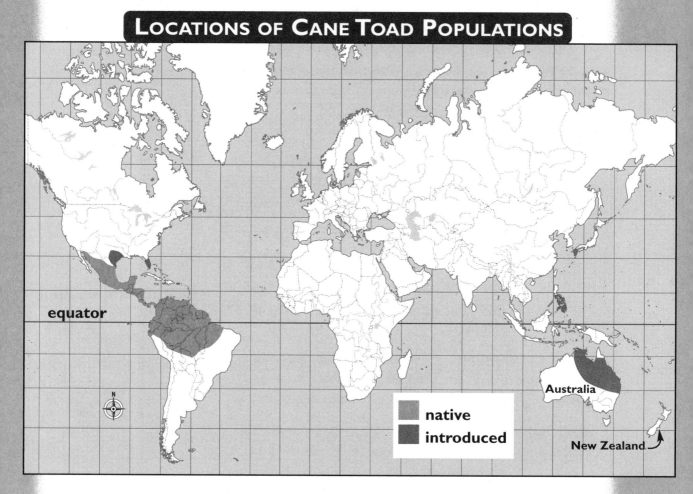

LOCATIONS OF CANE TOAD POPULATIONS

equator

Australia

New Zealand

native
introduced

▶ *What do all the cane toad locations have in common?*

_____

_____

▶ *Look at the map. What can you infer about the best climate for cane toads?*

_____

_____

THE POPULATION EXPLOSION Scientists studying cane toads have found that cane toad tadpoles hatch very quickly, most of the time within three days. The tadpoles also develop lungs and legs early, and so are able to leave the water and live on land sooner than most frogs' tadpoles.

▶ *How do these traits make the cane toad population very successful?*

_____

_____

_____

_____

_____

_____

▶ *Native frogs in Australia eat only certain types of food. But a cane toad will eat anything that moves past it and fits in its mouth. How could the cane toad's diet contribute to its success?*

_____

_____

_____

_____

_____

▶ Take Action

WRITE A LETTER You are working as an ecologist in Kakadu National Park in northern Australia. Cane toads have just begun to appear there. The toads migrated north from Queensland. One day, you receive a letter from another ecologist who works in a park in the southern part of New Zealand's South Island. She is worried that the cane toads will one day arrive on the South Island in boat cargo and travel to her park. Review the map and questions on the previous page. Write a letter to her on a separate piece of paper. Include information about cane toads, what risks they pose for your park, where they normally live, and the likelihood of cane toads invading her park.

Populations, Communities, and Ecosystems

Poison Toads

If you're big and slow, how can you escape hungry predators?

By most accounts, cane toads are big, slow, and ugly. They can grow up to 24 cm in length and weigh over 1 kg. Their rough, dry skin is covered with bumps that look like warts. But size and looks are not enough to scare away hungry predators that want to eat them. Cane toads have a special defense that protects them from many attackers in their communities.

 **Before You Read**

DESCRIBE A COMMUNITY Different populations living together in the same area form a community. A cane toad population lives among populations of native frogs, snakes, water rats, ibis, crows, and other organisms.

A common way populations of organisms in a community interact is by eating each other. For example, a mosquito population serves as food for the cane toad population. At the same time, the cane toad population serves as food for the population of Keelback snakes, which aren't affected by the toads' toxin. Snakes are eaten by foxes, dogs, and other animals.

▶ *Think about the community in which you live. Describe three animals' defenses that help them survive in your community.*

_____

_____

_____

_____

_____

_____

UNIT 5: ECOLOGY

182

NOTEZONE

Circle the ways a cane toad protects itself against other populations in its community.

Cane toads have an unusual—and deadly—way of defending themselves.

Cane Toad Venom

One of the most important factors in the success of the cane toad is that they are highly poisonous to eat, at every stage of their life cycle.

All frogs and toads may have enlarged chemical-secreting glands at particular points on their bodies, or small glands spread over the whole skin. The chemicals they produce…may be highly toxic. The cane toad is one such amphibian. A cane toad's reaction to a threat is to turn [so that] the venom glands face [the attacker]. Cane toad venom is also found all over their skin. Animals [that pick up] a cane toad [in their mouth] and [receive] a dose of venom may die within fifteen minutes.

The glands on the cane toads' shoulders are also capable of oozing venom or even squirting it over a distance of up to 2 m if the toad is particularly roughly treated.

…[Cane toads'] diet includes small lizards, frogs, mice and even younger cane toads. They have also been known to steal food from dog and cat bowls.

----

secreting: releasing
glands: organs that release chemicals used in other parts of the body
toxic: poisonous, deadly
amphibian: an animal that starts life in water and uses gills to breathe but lives on land, or both on land and in water, and uses lungs to breathe as an adult

venom: a poisonous substance released by an animal
dose: a specific quantity

From: "Cane Toads—Bufo Marinus." *Australian Museum Fact Sheets*. Australian Museum. (www.amonline.net.au/factsheets/canetoad.htm)

FIND OUT MORE

SCIENCESAURUS
Animal Life Cycles 106
Researching
Information   420

INTERACTIONS WITHIN A COMMUNITY The diagram at right shows the life cycle of the cane toad.

Adult cane toads with their developed venom glands are highly poisonous. But cane toads at other stages of their life cycle—including eggs, tadpoles, and young toads—are also poisonous.

▶ *Which other population might be affected by poisonous toad eggs in a pond? (Hint: What other animal shares the pond?) How would it be affected? What change might it produce?*

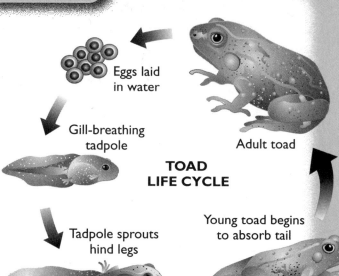

Eggs laid in water

Gill-breathing tadpole

Adult toad

TOAD LIFE CYCLE

Young toad begins to absorb tail

Tadpole sprouts hind legs

_____

_____

_____

_____

▶ *How might another population in the community such as egrets be affected by this change?*

_____

_____

_____

_____

◀ **Little egret**

▶ *Which other populations in the cane toad community might be affected directly or indirectly by the toad? Base your answer on the feeding relationships that exist within a community of animals.*

_____

_____

_____

▶ Propose Explanations

THINK ABOUT IT Based on what you know about cane toad venom and the diet of cane toads, what impact do you think invading cane toads have on native populations of animals living in the area?

_____

_____

_____

_____

▶ *Why do you think people are trying to reduce cane toad populations and keep them from spreading into new communities?*

_____

_____

▶ *How could you find out whether invading cane toads were affecting other populations in the community? Describe the kind of data you would gather and the period of time over which you would gather it.*

_____

_____

_____

_____

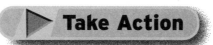

▶ Take Action

RESEARCH AN INVADING SPECIES The cane toad is not the only animal that has been introduced to a new area to solve a problem, only to end up causing new problems in the community.

▶ *What other animal populations have been introduced to new areas? Research one of the following introduced species, or choose another. Why was the species introduced? Was it introduced on purpose or by accident? How did the species affect the native populations in the community?*

- American bullfrog (*Rana catesbeiana*)
- House sparrow (*Passer domesticus*)
- Gypsy moth (*Lymantria dispar*)
- Zebra mussel (*Dreissena polymorpha*)
- Muskrat (*Ondatra zibethicus*)
- Starling (*Sturnus vulgaris*)

Populations, Communities, and Ecosystems

Bad Neighbors

Cane toads are everywhere! But are they a disaster or just a disruption?

Until cane toads were introduced in 1935, Australia didn't have any native toad species. The toads' impact on the ecosystems to which they spread was immediate and severe. The hungry toads wiped out food supplies, leaving many native frog species without anything to eat. They also posed a deadly threat to native predators that tried to eat them. But what are the long-term effects of a toad invasion?

AUSTRALIA

Darwin

QUEENSLAND

Brisbane

Perth

Adelaide
Canberra   Sydney
Melbourne

▶ **Read**

How severe is the cane toad threat? A land manager in Queensland, Australia, shares her observations.

Disaster or Disruption?

Chris Holt was invaded [by cane toads] twice…. A decade ago she and husband Malcolm owned Balbarini station…where they were attacked en masse. "They came by the road, not in the creeks as we had been told they would," she recalled. "It was just disgusting. The road was like a moving carpet at night. It was as if they sent in big shock troops because some of the ones at the front were as big as bread and butter plates. They were huge." Ms. Holt remembers the initial effects were devastating. "We found lots of dead freshwater crocodiles in the shallow water holes in the river. We found dead goannas and had no snakes at all that year."

She said the tree frogs nearly disappeared, but by the end of the dry [season] the toads had no more food and the Holts found themselves surrounded by dead cane toads…. The Holt family…watched as native species managed to survive. "The native animals seem to learn

FIND OUT MORE

SCIENCESAURUS

Animal Behavior	110
Ecosystems	129
Relationships Between Populations	132

SCI**LINKS**
THE WORLD'S A CLICK AWAY

www.scilinks.org
Keyword: Populations, Communities, and Ecosystems
Code: GSLD22

quite quickly that you can't eat them," explains Ms. Holt. "In our experience [the cane toads] had no long-term effect on the wildlife whatsoever."

Many of those living in the Gulf region report how quickly predatory birds learned to adjust to the poison sacs the cane toads carry on their backs. "The crows and kites have learned to live with them," says [Louise] Martin. "They pick the cane toads up and turn them over and pick their guts out."

en masse: in a large group

shock troops: soldiers specially trained to lead an attack

initial: first

goannas: Australian monitor lizards

predatory: hunting and eating other organisms

kites: birds that eat small animals, including toads

From: Schulz, Dennis. "The Cane Toad Dialogues: Disaster or Disruption?" *Tropical Savannas Cooperative Research Centre.* Northern Territory University. (savanna.ntu.edu.au/publications/savanna_links16/toad.html)

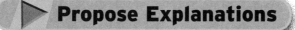

▶ Propose Explanations

THE END OF THE EXPLOSION Which nonliving part of the cane toad's ecosystem is most changed by a cane toad population? How do you think this might in turn affect other populations in the ecosystem?

_____

_____

_____

▶ *Why do you think the cane toad population at Balbarini station increased so rapidly at first?*

_____

_____

▶ *What factors do you think might contribute to the decline of a cane toad population after several months or years?*

_____

_____

_____

EAT OR BE EATEN

In the desert grasslands of southern Arizona, life-and-death struggles happen every day.

Carl and Jane Bock are scientists who have studied the Sonoita grasslands for more than 20 years. They were interested in learning about the trials that living things face in this dry, southeastern Arizona area. One of their areas of study was predator-prey relationships, especially among coyotes and rodents such as rats and mice. First, the Bocks learned all they could about coyotes, in both legend and science. They observed coyotes and rodents in the wild. Then they conducted experiments to learn more about how predators and their prey interact.

▶ Before You Read

THINK ABOUT IT Every ecosystem is a study in survival. Animals must constantly look for food and avoid being food for something else. Plants (producers) make food by photosynthesis. Plant-eaters (herbivores) eat plants. Meat-eaters (carnivores) eat herbivores. Carnivores are also called predators, and the animals they eat are their prey.

Any series of eating relationships is called a food chain. Grass ➝ mouse ➝ snake ➝ hawk is an example of a food chain. The arrows point from the organism being eaten to the organism doing the eating. In nature, many food chains usually overlap to create a food web.

Think of the wild organisms in your area. Who eats what? What would happen to the prey if its predators were removed?

_____

_____

DRAW A FOOD CHAIN Show the feeding relationships between some wild organisms that live in your area. Label the producers, herbivores, and carnivores. Then label the predators and prey.

Read

NOTE ZONE

Circle the producers and underline the prey.

Here is what the Bocks observed about how coyotes and rodents interact.

The View from Bald Hill

Few animals provoke such strong and varied opinions as coyotes. They are "ruthless" if they kill livestock and they are "useful" if they kill mice and jackrabbits that otherwise might "overrun the range."

Coyotes, of course, are neither ruthless or useful. They just are, and at the Research Ranch they were welcomed as part of the natural scene. We found dens...where coyotes raised their pups, some surprisingly close to roads and houses. Coyotes hunt the mesas and washes at dawn and at dusk, mostly alone but sometimes in pairs. They watched us as intently as we watched them and usually did not run unless we got too close.

When we examined coyote scat, we found the digested remains of desert cottontails, black-tailed jackrabbits, rock squirrels, pocket mice, woodrats, harvest mice, cotton rats, white-tailed deer, mule deer, pronghorn, peccaries, cattle, grasshoppers, beetles, moths, spiders, sparrows, lizards, grass, acorns, juniper seeds, cactus fruits, and mesquite beans.

---

ruthless: without mercy
mesa: flat-topped elevation of land
wash: often dry bed of a creek or small river
scat: animal droppings, feces

From: Bock, Carl E., and Jane H. Bock. *The View from Bald Hill: Thirty Years in an Arizona Grassland.* University of California Press.

FIND OUT MORE

SCIENCE SAURUS

Populations	130
Ecosystems	131
Relationships Between Populations	132
Feeding Relationships	133
Food Chains	134
Food Webs	135

SCI LINKS.
THE WORLD'S A CLICK AWAY

www.scilinks.org
Keyword: Food Webs
Code: GSLD23

FORM A HYPOTHESIS The Bocks counted and recorded the number of rodents in an area of the Research Ranch for three years. Then they asked, "What would happen to the number of rodents if coyotes were eliminated from one area of the Research Ranch?" After asking the question, they formed a hypothesis—a prediction that can be tested.

▶ *Form your own hypothesis to answer the question. Use an "if / then" sentence: IF something happens, THEN something else will happen.*

_____

_____

The Bocks hypothesized that if they eliminated coyotes and other predators from one area, then the number of prey animals in that area would increase. The Bocks carried out experiments to test their hypothesis. In one such experiment in 1989, they counted and recorded the number of rodents trapped in two areas of the Research Ranch. One area was open to predators. The other area was fenced off so that large predators could not eat any of the rodents, but the rodents could enter and exit the fenced-off area.

The Bocks set out thousands of traps during the year. Each trap set out overnight was called one "trap-night." They recorded the number of rodents that were trapped, then calculated the average number caught per 100 trap-nights. The following graph shows their results.

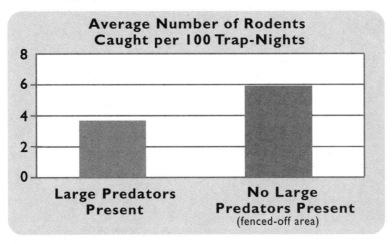

ANALYZE THE DATA
▶ *Examine the results shown on the graph. Do the data support your hypothesis? Explain your answer using the data.*

_____

_____

_____

Propose Explanations

WHAT DO YOU THINK? Based on the Bocks' results, what conclusion could they draw about coyotes and rodents in the Research Ranch ecosystem?

_____

_____

_____

▶ *What could be the reasons for the difference in the number of rodents in the fenced and unfenced areas? Try to think of as many reasons as you can.*

_____

_____

_____

IDENTIFY VARIABLES
▶ *What factors other than predators would affect how many rodents are in the area? (Hint: What do rodents need to survive?)*

_____

_____

_____

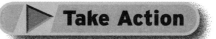

Take Action

DO RESEARCH Form groups in your class and choose an animal from the list below. Then do research to find out if any local or state agencies have plans to eliminate or control that animal. Based on what you've read about coyotes and rodents, describe the effect that killing the animal you chose would have on the ecosystem in which it lives.

Raccoons	Rats	Crows	Skunks	Foxes
Deer	Opossums	Pigeons	Woodchucks	Mice
Alligators	Snakes	Buzzards	Squirrels	

_____

_____

_____

A Place of Their Own

In any ecosystem, many different organisms interact with each other. With limited resources, how do they all survive?

Every ecosystem has resources such as food sources and water. Only a certain amount of those resources is available. The Bocks asked a scientific question: How do so many things live together in an area with limited resources? In the area of the Research Ranch, the Bocks observed a number of species of sparrows and similar birds. Then they collected data that told them about the relationships between the birds and the factors in their environment, including food and nesting sites.

NOTEZONE

Underline the two possible reasons that the different bird species live in different habitats.

▶ **Read**

Here are more of the Bocks' observations.

The View from Bald Hill

Sparrows are among the dullest of birds. Nearly all are brown and gray, and they spend most of their lives on the ground, quietly searching for seeds and insects while avoiding being eaten themselves. They are distinctive only when they sing to proclaim their territories and attract mates. Yet, sparrows have much to tell us about the ecology of grassland communities of which they are a part.

A dozen species of ground-dwelling and seed-eating songbirds winter regularly on the Research Ranch. Six of them are migratory and come only in winter, five are residents year round, and one is sometimes there in both winter and summer. The twelve species divide up the habitats in generally predictable ways, regardless of their numbers from one year to the next. Avian ecologists have arrived at two different explanations for the patterns they found. First, it may be the result of competition for the limited seed supply they all share.

FIND OUT MORE

SCIENCESAURUS

Factors That Affect
Populations   131
Relationships
Between
Populations   132

Perhaps each species forages most efficiently and successfully in a particular habitat and aggressively keeps other species away. A second possibility is that the birds are choosing those habitats where they are best able to avoid being eaten by predators.

distinctive: noticeably different
proclaim: declare publicly
winter: spend the winter in a place
migratory: living in different places at different times of the year
avian: relating to birds
forage: search for food

From: Bock, Carl E., and Jane H. Bock. *The View from Bald Hill: Thirty Years in an Arizona Grassland.* University of California Press.

White-crowned sparrow ▼

▶ **Explore**

ANALYZE DATA The Bocks predicted that different species of birds live in different habitats within the grassland ecosystem. To test their prediction, the Bocks set up observation stations in many different kinds of habitats on the Research Ranch. Then they observed and recorded the species of birds that appeared in each habitat. Study the table below. It shows where sparrows and other small seed-eating birds live within the ecosystem of the Research Ranch.

Species	Major Habitat
White-crowned sparrow	Heavy brush along drainages
Rufous-crowned sparrow	Shrubby ravines and tall grasslands
Canyon towee	Woodlands and shrublands
Chipping sparrow	Oak woodland
Vesper sparrow	Shrubby grasslands
Savannah sparrow	Shrubby grasslands
Cassin's sparrow	Shrubby grasslands
Eastern meadowlark	Grasslands with variable cover
Grasshopper sparrow	Open grasslands, heavy grass cover
Baird's sparrow	Open grasslands, heavy grass cover
Horned lark	Open grasslands with bare ground
Chestnut collared longspur	Open grasslands with bare ground

brush: low vegetation
drainage: area of land that drains surface water
ravine: narrow, steep valley

DRAW CONCLUSIONS Based on their observations, the Bocks concluded that the 12 species of birds can all survive in the ecosystem because they live in different habitats. Explain how the data in the table on page 193 support and do not support the Bocks' conclusion.

_____

_____

_____

▶ **Propose Explanations**

FILLING A NICHE Each species fills its own niche—or territory—within a habitat. For a bird, its niche provides what it needs: the food it requires, an escape from predators, and a place to nest. Some bird species have different requirements, but others compete for the same things. If two species need the same resources, the more aggressive species will usually force the weaker one out.

▶ _How could different niches make it possible for the vesper sparrow and Cassin's sparrow to live in the same habitat?_

_____

_____

_____

The Bocks performed another experiment. They put piles of branches around the Research Ranch where there weren't any before and observed what happened. They found that grasshopper sparrows and horned larks left the area while some chipping sparrows arrived. Vesper sparrows became the most common bird species in the area.

▶ _Refer to the table again. Why did the chipping sparrows and vesper sparrows arrive?_

_____

_____

▶ _Given what you learned about niches, what is a possible reason the grasshopper sparrows and horned larks left?_

_____

_____

MAKE PREDICTIONS What if all the trees in the study area were cut down? Based on the data in the table, predict what would happen to the populations of canyon towees and chipping sparrows.

_____

_____

HAVE A DEBATE A construction company wants to build a mall on some land outside your town. Right now, the land is filled with weeds and shrubs. The mall would have more than 60 stores that will bring more business into your town. It will also provide hundreds of jobs for local residents. Use the spaces below to write your arguments for and against building the mall.

Class Debate Side 1: Argue in favor of building the mall.

_____

_____

_____

_____

_____

_____

Class Debate Side 2: Argue against building the mall.

_____

_____

_____

_____

_____

_____

▲
**Chipping
sparrow**

Under the Grassland Sky

The Fragile Land

A healthy ecosystem supports a diversity of life. Even suburbs, cities, and towns have ecosystems that can be disturbed. What about the one where you live?

Human beings share an environment with many other organisms. Unlike the animals studied by the Bocks, our food and shelter often come from far-away places. Even so, we have a big impact on our surrounding ecosystems.

▶ **Explore**

DIAGRAM YOUR ECOSYSTEM Think about where you live. Like the Sonoita grasslands, your suburb, city, or town is filled with living things that are all trying to survive.

▶ *Construct a food web of the plants and animals where you live. Also include food sources that arrive from outside the ecosystem. Draw an arrow from each organism to every other organism that eats it.*

FIND OUT MORE

SCIENCESAURUS

Ecosystems   131
Factors That Affect
  Populations   131
Relationships
  Between
  Populations   132
Feeding
  Relationships   133
Food Webs   135

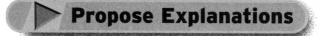

▶ Propose Explanations

CHANGES MADE BY HUMANS Humans often make changes that affect the ecosystem. We build structures like roads, houses, dams, and bridges to make our environment more livable for ourselves. But these changes may make the environment a less friendly place for other organisms.

▶ *List several structures in your ecosystem that were made by people.*

_____

_____

_____

▶ *How do you think these structures might threaten some animals and plants in your area? How might these structures be useful to animals and plants?*

_____

_____

_____

▶ Take Action

MAKE ROOM FOR ALL Your town needs new housing for 100 families. As a member of the Environmental Planning Commission, you want to make sure the building plan disrupts the ecosystem as little as possible.

Create a checklist for developers to fill out in order to get permission to build. Think of the types of organisms in your environment and the nonliving factors they depend on for survival. What recommendations would you make to protect plant and animal species and the environment they depend on for food and shelter?

_____

_____

_____

_____

_____

_____

Let It Rain

The tapir may look unusual, but it is well adapted to survive in the Amazon rain forest.

Tropical rain forests are very wet and very warm. Average yearly rainfall is 200–450 cm, and the average temperature is about 25°C all year long. These warm, wet conditions provide a lush environment for thousands of unique plant and animal species.

▶ Before You Read

TAKING MEASUREMENTS See how much rain actually falls in a tropical rain forest each year. Measure the rainfall on a long strip of adding machine tape. Use a meter stick or a metric tape measure to measure 200 cm and 450 cm from one end of the strip. Mark and label each measurement.

Next, use a world almanac or the Internet to find the average rainfall each year in your area. (It may be called average precipitation.) Write that information below. Then measure and mark your area's rainfall on the strip.

Average yearly rainfall in my area: _____

▶ *How does the yearly rainfall in your area compare with the yearly rainfall in a tropical rain forest?*

_____

_____

_____

_____

Which animals are the tapir related to?

▶ **Read**

The tapir is one of the more unusual mammals found in a tropical rain forest.

A Rain Forest Resident

The lowland tapir [is] found in [tropical rain] forests from northern Colombia to northern Argentina....

Tapirs are the only [living] native American members of *Perissodactyla*, the ancient order to which horses and rhinoceroses belong. Like their relatives, they are far from dainty, averaging six feet (195 cm) long and three feet (85 cm) high and weighing about 440 pounds (200 kg). At one end of their hefty, rotund bodies are short, stumpy tails. At the other [end are] elongated upper lips that curve down like abbreviated elephant trunks. They use this flexible proboscis as a dining tool, sniffing out and sweeping tasty vegetation and fruits into their mouths.

With which animal does it share a similar feature, and what is that feature?

They are an endangered species because their forest habitats are rapidly being logged and developed, they reproduce slowly,...and they are hugely popular game animals....

dainty: delicate
hefty: big and heavy
rotund: round, plump
stumpy: short and thick
elongated: having more length than width

abbreviated: shortened
proboscis: a long, flexible snout
game animals: wild animals that are hunted for sport or food

From: Medici, Patricia, and J. Pablo Juliá. "Scientists Trap, Tag, And Track Tapirs To Design A Survival Strategy." *Eco-Exchange.* Rainforest Alliance.
(ra.org/programs/cmc/newsletter/nov01-2.html)

FIND OUT MORE

SCIENCESAURUS
Biomes   141
Tropical Rain
   Forests   145
Pattern of World
   Climates   230

Baby tapir ▶

THINK ABOUT IT Adaptations are physical or behavioral features that help a species survive and reproduce in its environment. For example, adaptations might help a species gather food, escape from predators, catch prey, locate and attract others of its species, or survive harsh conditions such as extreme heat or cold.

Based on fossil evidence, scientists have concluded that the tapir's physical features and behavior haven't changed much over the last 20 million years.

▶ *What does this tell you about the tapir's habitat long ago?*

_____

_____

_____

_____

_____

Like its ancient ancestors, the tapir today is a large, heavy animal with a long snout, powerful jaws, excellent swimming skills, and a vegetarian diet. Because of its heavy, round body, you might think that the tapir is easily caught by predators. Actually, when a tapir is threatened, it can escape quickly by running into thick, low brush. If it is near a body of water, it can escape by swimming away.

MAKE INFERENCES Look at the chart on the next page. The left column identifies many of the tapir's adaptations. Using what you've read so far and what you know about other animals, fill in the right side of the chart. Explain how each adaptation might help tapirs survive. The first answer is done for you.

Adult tapir ▲

Adaptations of the Tapir	How These Adaptations Help the Tapir Survive in the Rain Forest
long, flexible snout that can pull and move objects	helps push food into its mouth
thick, hard, tough skin	
powerful jaws	
large size; great strength; powerful legs	
strong swimmer; can even walk along the bottom of streams and rivers	
Baby tapirs have striped and spotted coats.	

▶ **Take Action**

AMAZON ADAPTATIONS Research another animal that lives in the tropical rain forests of South America. Identify some of the animal's adaptations. Explain how each adaptation helps it survive. Present your findings in a chart similar to the tapir chart on this page.

Rain Forest

The Seeds of Biodiversity

As tapirs eat their way through the rain forest, they help preserve it.

Patricia Medici and Juan Pablo Juliá are South American scientists who study the lowland tapir. Together, they work on Project Tapir, a research project to learn about the behavior of this strange-looking creature. Their goal is to figure out how to save the endangered tapir from extinction. They also study how to protect the wide variety, or diversity, of species that live in the rain forest.

Project Tapir began in 1996 in Morro do Diabo State Park near São Paulo, Brazil. Medici estimates that there are about 400 tapirs in this wildlife preserve. She and Juliá have trapped, collared, and tracked 18 tapirs during the past five years. Through their studies, they have learned a great deal about the tapirs' habits and movements.

SOUTH AMERICA

BRAZIL

Morro do Diabo State Park

São Paulo

▶ **Before You Read**

SPECIES INTERACT Select a wild animal that lives in your area. Describe some of the ways that this animal interacts with other organisms and with nonliving things in its natural environment. How could you find out more about your animal's behavior?

▶ **Read**

NOTEZONE

Without tapirs, how do you think the seeds of the fruit trees in the rain forest would be scattered?

Tapirs cannot digest the seeds in the fruit they eat. This is good news for the rain forest!

How Tapirs Spread Seeds

Tapirs are extremely important to the health and biodiversity of tropical forests, because they are among the best agents of seed dispersal. Like [many] other mammals that are herbivores, they lack the enzymes that can digest plant cellulose, so their stomachs have separate chambers where microorganisms live and digest the vegetation. Since this isn't a very efficient system, they must [eat] large quantities of plants and fruits for sufficient energy....

[Then, the tapir expels large] amounts of droppings, which are loaded with seeds and other undigested material. Seeds dropped by roaming tapirs grow into the same plants and trees that provide future tapirs—and of course, many other animals—with future meals and shelter. "Morro do Diabo would be a very different forest if we didn't have tapirs," [biologist Patricia] Medici acknowledges.

biodiversity: the variety of species in an environment
agents: causes
dispersal: scattering
herbivores: animals that eat only plants
enzymes: chemicals in the digestive system that help break down food
cellulose: tough fibers found in plants
chambers: sections

Tapir ▲

From: Medici, Patricia, and J. Pablo Juliá. "Scientists Trap, Tag, And Track Tapirs To Design A Survival Strategy." *Eco-Exchange*. Rainforest Alliance. (ra.org/programs/cmc/newsletter/nov01-2.html)

FIND OUT MORE

SCIENCESAURUS
Biodiversity 124
Tropical Rain Forests 145

TAPIR TRACKS To learn about the tapir, Juliá and Medici tracked its paths through the forest. From careful observation, they learned some surprising information about this species' habits. Medici likes to describe the tapirs as "landscape detectives" because their movements show conservationists exactly which parts of the rain forest need protection.

Palm fruits are one of the tapir's favorite foods. It must eat large quantities of these plants to survive. Palm fruits are also a popular food for humans in the area. But the trunk of the palm tree is hard and slippery, making it difficult to climb. So, to get the fruit, the people chop down the trees. In contrast, when the tapirs eat the fruit that falls from the trees, they help spread the palm fruit's seeds. Some of the seeds will eventually grow into new trees.

▶ *If the tapir became extinct, what do you think would happen to the palm trees? Why?*

_____

_____

_____

_____

▶ *Tapirs are hunted and eaten by jaguars, crocodiles, and people. How would these predators be affected if the tapir became extinct?*

_____

_____

_____

_____

▶ Propose Explanations

POPULATION DENSITY Other scientists have tracked the tapir population on Barro Colorado Island in Panama. The graph on the next page shows the density of the tapir population from 1920 to 1990. "Density" means the average number of tapirs per square kilometer of forest.

▶ *When did the tapir species come closest to extinction in this area? Explain why.*

_____

_____

▶ *When did the tapir's numbers increase, and why?*

_____

_____

_____

_____

_____

_____

_____

_____

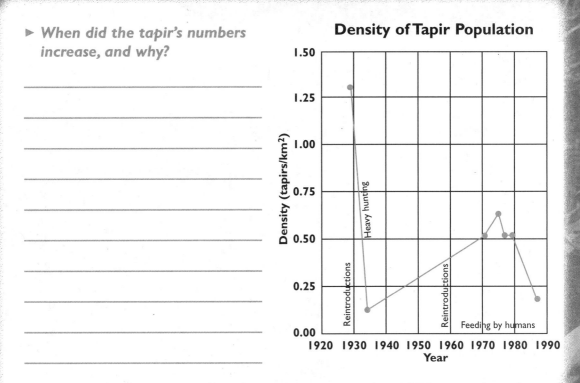

Density of Tapir Population

▶ *The tapir's numbers decreased sharply again after 1975, even though people were feeding them. What might have caused this decline? (Hint: Review the reading on page 199.)*

_____

_____

_____

_____

▶ Take Action

FUNDING THE RAIN FOREST Imagine you are a scientist researching an animal that lives in the rain forest. Choose the rain forest animal you would like to study. Then write a proposal to the National Science Foundation (NSF) requesting funding to carry out your research. Include the following in your proposal:

• a description of the animal
• why you want to study it
• what makes it an important research subject
• how it lives in its habitat (what it eats, how it moves around, how it escapes predators)
• why you need funding to carry out your research

Rain Forest

Going, Going...Gone?

Earth's most complex ecosystems—tropical rain forests—are rapidly being destroyed by human activity.

During the 1990s, more than 15 million hectares (almost 58,000 square miles) of tropical rain forest were lost every year. At that rate, all of Earth's tropical rain forests could be gone in only 75 to 100 years.

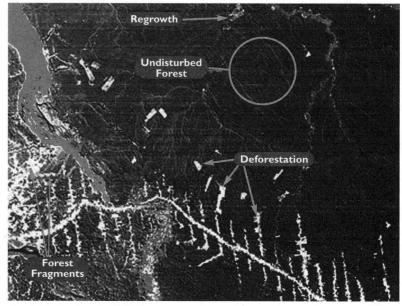

▲ Satellite image of rain forest in Brazil

Explore

PICTURES FROM SPACE How do scientists know how much rain forest has been destroyed? The National Aeronautics and Space Administration (NASA) has been studying rain forest destruction for many years. NASA uses satellites orbiting Earth to take pictures of rain forests around the world. By analyzing these images, scientists can tell how much of a rain forest has been cleared and how much remains.

▶ *Examine the satellite image above. Areas of rain forest that have been cleared are shown in white. What do you think the straight white lines represent?*

WHY DO PEOPLE CLEAR RAIN FORESTS? Three types of human activities are responsible for most rain forest destruction—farming, cattle ranching, and logging. Here are some questions you might want to investigate.

▶ *Most rain forest land is cleared using a method called slash and burn. What is slash and burn? How does it damage the land? When can it actually be good for the land?*

UNIT 5: ECOLOGY

- ▶ *What is subsistence farming? Why do so many local people need to clear land to raise crops? How do subsistence farmers help take care of the land?*
- ▶ *Loggers use selective cutting to obtain valuable wood such as mahogany and teak. What is selective cutting? How does it help preserve a rain forest? How does it damage the forest?*
- ▶ *Who buys the meat from cattle that were raised on ranches cleared from tropical rain forests?*

WHAT ARE SOME OTHER CHOICES? Conservationists, government officials, and local people are working together. They are trying to find ways to preserve rain forests and still meet people's needs. You might want to investigate these questions.

- ▶ *What is ecotourism? How does it help preserve rain forests? In what ways can it damage a rain forest? How does it benefit a nation's economy? How does it benefit local people?*
- ▶ *What does sustainable harvesting mean? How does it help preserve rain forests? How do local people benefit? What types of resources are harvested?*
- ▶ *What is shade agriculture? Which types of plants can be grown using this farming method?*

▶ **Take Action**

FINDING ANSWERS Decide on a rain forest topic that interests you. Choose one or more of the questions posed in this lesson, or think of your own questions. Use the library or Internet resources to find the answers to the questions.

Cleared rain forest ▶

Protecting Earth

The Lesson of Easter Island

Hundreds of giant stone statues are scattered across Easter Island. They are the remains of a society that once thrived on the island.

Easter Island is a tiny island in the Pacific Ocean, known best for its many ancient stone statues. The island is very isolated. It is more than 2,000 miles (3,200 km) from the nearest continent, South America, and 1,400 miles (2,240 km) from the nearest island where people live. The first people on Easter Island probably arrived around 400 A.D. At that time, the island was covered by lush subtropical forests. Eventually, as many as 20,000 people lived there.

Today there are no trees over 10 feet (3 m) tall on the island, and it is home to only about 2,000 people. Researchers who studied Easter Island discovered that the ancient society used up the island's resources. They wiped out the forests and drove plants and animals to extinction. Evidence shows this happened in just a few hundred years. The loss of resources led to the destruction of the island society.

Before You Read

GENERATE IDEAS The stone statues on Easter Island are as tall as 66 feet (20 m) and weigh up to 270 tons (245 metric tons). The islanders carved the statues in one place and then moved them to other places. Yet, the people didn't have the heavy equipment we have today—only trees, shrubs, vines, and their own muscle power. They did not even have horses or other large animals!

▶ *How might the islanders have moved the statues?*

_____

_____

_____

_____

_____

_____

Read

NOTEZONE

Circle the reasons why the population began to crash.

It took only a few hundred years for the people of Easter Island to destroy the island's environment.

Easter's End

[Easter Island's] growing population was cutting the forest more rapidly than the forest was regenerating. The people used the land for gardens and the wood for fuel, canoes, and houses—and...for lugging statues. As the forest disappeared, the islanders ran out of timber and rope to transport and [set up] their statues. Life became more uncomfortable—springs and streams dried up, and wood was no longer available for fires.

People also found it harder to fill their stomachs, as land birds, large sea snails, and many seabirds disappeared. Because timber for building seagoing canoes vanished, fish catches declined and porpoises disappeared from the table. Crop yields also declined, since deforestation allowed the soil to be eroded by rain and wind [and] dried by the sun....

▲ Statues on Easter Island

By around 1700, the population began to crash toward between one-quarter and one-tenth of its former number.... Rival clans started to [push over] each other's statues, breaking the heads off....

As we...imagine the decline of Easter's civilization, we ask ourselves, "Why didn't they...realize what they were doing and stop before it was too late?"

---

regenerating: growing again
lugging: dragging
timber: wood
crop yields: fruit and vegetable harvests

deforestation: destruction of the forest
eroded: washed or blown away
rival: competing

From: Diamond, Jared. "Easter's End." *Discover*

FIND OUT MORE

SCIENCESAURUS
Ecosystems   129
Populations   130
Factors That Affect
Populations   131

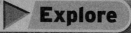 **Explore**

COMPARE EASTER ISLAND AND YOUR COMMUNITY Easter

Island serves as a model of what can happen when humans destroy their environment. Think of places in your community where the natural environment has been changed due to human use such as building roads, dams, and other structures. To compare Easter Island with your community, fill in the chart below. In the first column, identify something humans did that changed the environment on Easter Island. In the second column, identify something humans have done that changed the environment in your community. In the next three columns, compare the types of change in the two places. One example is done for you.

Environmental change on Easter Island	Environmental change in my community	Change: same or different?	Reason for change	Effect of environmental change
Cut down trees	Cut down trees	same	Easter Island: to get fuel My community: to build a skating rink	Easter Island: Eventually there were no trees left. My community: There's no shade to keep the area cool.

▶ *Do you think the Easter Island example can help us predict what could happen in other places on Earth? Why or why not?*

_____

_____

_____

_____

_____

▶ Propose Explanations

USE WHAT YOU KNOW

▶ Why didn't the people of Easter Island trade with other people to get the things they needed? (Hint: Look at the map on page 208.)

_____

_____

▶ Why didn't the people of Easter Island move to another place?

_____

_____

▶ What do you think the people of Easter Island could have done to avoid destroying their environment?

_____

_____

_____

_____

▶ Take Action

COMPARE AND CONTRAST Do research to learn more about Easter Island. Then fill in the Venn diagram below to compare Easter Island before and after deforestation. On the left side, describe Easter Island before deforestation. On the right side, describe Easter Island after deforestation. In the center, list the ways that the island stayed the same.

BEFORE   SAME   AFTER

Protecting Earth

People Make a Difference

People have the power to destroy ecosystems or preserve them.

Swamps, marshes, and other aquatic ecosystems may seem like unimportant places, but they help prevent floods and are home to a great diversity of life. They are also some of the most easily damaged ecosystems on Earth.

NOTEZONE

Underline the ways that humans damage or destroy aquatic ecosystems.

▶ Read

Our need for electric power, factories, and roads has a large impact on aquatic ecosystems.

Human Impacts

How do humans affect aquatic ecosystems?

Probably, people don't really say, "Let's go out and destroy an aquatic ecosystem just for fun." Instead they say, "I want to do such-and-such and, if an aquatic ecosystem is harmed in the process, well, that's the price of progress. Life is full of compromises."

We plan change and construction to [adjust to] population growth, industry, and demand for electric power. All too often that construction involves draining swamps to "reclaim" dry land, building protective levees, [and] keeping shipping channels dredged…. [It also often involves] building dams for hydroelectric power, building canals, laying water pipes, and carrying out other projects. These activities are carried out by local…agencies…and/or federal units, such as the U.S. Army Corps of Engineers. The projects serve to build communities, redirect water for farms, [and] prevent floods…. [The] projects provide water supplies, support transportation, and [serve] other functions related to the "progress" of humans.

aquatic: relating to water
compromise: giving in partway in order to settle differences
reclaim: return something to an earlier condition for use
levee: a raised area alongside a river to keep it from overflowing

shipping channel: the deeper part of a river or harbor
dredged: deepened a waterway by removing mud from the bottom
hydroelectric power: electricity that is generated by using the energy of moving water

FIND OUT MORE

SCIENCESAURUS

Freshwater
  Ecosystems   148
Saltwater
  Ecosystems   149
Renewable Energy
  Resources   328
Habitat Loss   341

UNIT 5: ECOLOGY

From: Reynolds, Karen. "Human Impacts 101." *JASON Academy*. National Science Teacher's Association. (www.nsta.org/361/)

Explore

USING A GRAPH Why are human activities damaging aquatic ecosystems so much more now than in the past? One major reason is that the world's human population is so much larger today than in the past. This graph shows the growth of Earth's human population during the past 2,000 years.

▶ *About how large was the world's human population in each of the following years?*

750 A.D. _____

1500 A.D. _____

2000 A.D. _____

▶ *During the past 250 years, what happened to the rate of world population growth?*

_____

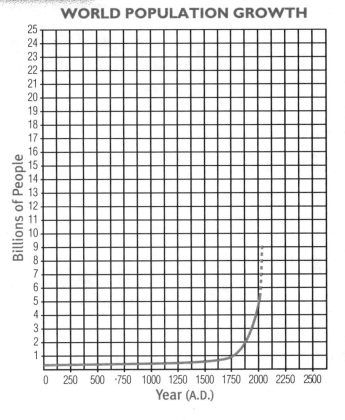

WORLD POPULATION GROWTH

Billions of People (y-axis: 1–25)

Year (A.D.) (x-axis: 0, 250, 500, 750, 1000, 1250, 1500, 1750, 2000, 2250, 2500)

▶ *Extend the line on the graph to the year 2250. If this growth rate continues, how large will the world's human population be in 2250? How will the size of the population in 2250 compare with the size of today's population?*

_____

_____

▶ *As the world human population grows, what is likely to happen to aquatic ecosystems? Why?*

_____

_____

_____

_____

_____

Protecting Earth

Be an Eco-Hero

**Humans don't live on this planet alone.
We are just one among millions of species.**

Some scientists suggest that humans face three major threats to survival. One is nuclear war. Another is worldwide climate change. The third is the loss of biodiversity on this planet. The word *biodiversity* means the incredible variety of organisms on Earth. There are more kinds of living things than you know!

▶ **Before You Read**

THINK ABOUT IT Many people try to save large animals such as pandas and elephants. However, most organisms are much smaller and less noticeable. Many people don't know about them or think about them. But species are disappearing from Earth at a rapid rate.

▶*If you had to choose between saving pandas and saving a species of small worms, which would you choose? Why?*

_____

_____

_____

_____

_____

_____

_____

_____

_____

_____

UNIT 5: ECOLOGY

▶ Read

Terry Erwin is a scientist from the Smithsonian Institution in Washington, D.C. Erwin found that in Panama, an incredible diversity of organisms live in a population of 19 trees of the same species.

Living Treasure

Scientists are dazzled and puzzled by the diversity of life on Earth. No one knows how many different kinds of plants, animals, and other organisms there are. But we do know that the organisms identified so far are only a small fraction of all living things....

And biologists have a name for...Earth's incredible variety of life: biodiversity....

Since [the 1700s], more than 1.5 million...species have been discovered and named.

On...[19] trees alone, [Terry Erwin] found more than 12,000 different kinds of beetles. He estimated that one out of seven species lived on that kind of tree and no other....

Until the 1980s, biologists estimated that 3 to 5 million species live on Earth. However, since large numbers of tropical insects and other organisms may live on just one kind of tree, or in one small area of tropical forest, the biodiversity of Earth may be much greater. Terry Erwin has estimated that...Earth may be home to 30 million species of insects alone.

biodiversity: the variety of living organisms in a given area

From: Pringle, Laurence. *Living Treasure: Saving Earth's Threatened Biodiversity.* HarperCollins Children's Books.

NOTEZONE

How many species have been discovered and named?

How many insect species does Terry Erwin estimate live on Earth?

About how many beetle species did Erwin estimate live only on those 19 trees?

FIND OUT MORE

SCIENCESAURUS
Biodiversity   124

www.scilinks.org
Keyword: Maintaining Biodiversity
Code: GSLD25

North America

Panama

South America

BIODIVERSITY IN YOUR WORLD

You do not need to go to a tropical forest to discover biodiversity. All you have to do is look carefully around you.

What You Need:

- meterstick or metric tape measure
- 12 sticks about 10–15 cm long
- string, 25 m
- notebook
- pencil
- large sheet of plain white paper
- trowel or large spoon
- index cards
- hand lens

What to Do:

1. Choose an area that appears to have more than one kind of plant in it. Measure a square that is 3 meters long on each side. Put sticks into the ground to mark the corners. Use string to show the sides.
2. Use the string and the other sticks to divide the square into 9 smaller squares that are 1 meter on each side.
3. In your notebook, make a map of your study plot. Include important features such as large rocks or water.
4. Examine your plot for any living things. Look everywhere—under rocks and logs, on tree trunks and branches, and on plant stems and leaves. Remember that the trees and other plants are living things, too! Use the hand lens to find very small organisms.
5. Dig up some soil and spread it out on the large sheet of paper. Include some decaying leaves, too. Use the hand lens to look for small organisms.
6. On index cards, sketch each kind of organism you found. Number each card. Record the number on your map to show where the organism was found.
7. Include signs of animals such as nests, animal tracks, feathers, cocoons, droppings, and spider webs. Draw each one on an index card. Letter each card, and record the letters on your map.

What Did You Find?

▶ *How many different kinds of organisms or signs of organisms did you find?*

_____

▶ *Do you think you found every kind of organism living in that plot?*

_____

▶ *What are some things you did or didn't do that might have kept you from finding some organisms?*

_____

_____

_____

_____

ANALYZE YOUR OBSERVATIONS

▶ *Examine your map and index cards. How were the organisms spaced around your plot?*

_____

_____

_____

▶ *Compare different parts of your plot. Where did you find the most biodiversity? Where did you find the least biodiversity?*

_____

_____

_____

▶ *What characteristics of your plot might have limited its biodiversity?*

_____

_____

► Take Action

Compare the results of your study with what others found in their plots. How are the findings similar? How are they different? Research the importance of biodiversity. How might the biodiversity you found benefit the wildlife in the area? What can you do to help maintain the biodiversity in your community? Write a report to share with the class.

Glossary of Scientific Terms

A

adaptation: structure, behavior, or other trait in an organism that helps it to survive in its environment

adaptive radiation: an evolutionary pattern in which related species become dissimilar, or less alike

adolescence: the teenage years

amphibian: animal that lives both on land and in water; Amphibians begin life in water with gills, but have lungs and breathe air as adults

antibody: protein made by the body that fights against a certain disease-causing substance

atom: smallest particle into which an element can be divided and still have the properties of that element

B

bacteria: one-celled organism that lacks a true nucleus

bar graph: graph that uses bars of different lengths to compare data

behavior: an activity or action that generally helps an organism survive in its environment

biodiversity: the variety of organisms in a specific environment or on Earth as a whole

biology: study of living things

blood: a tissue made up of cells and pieces of cells carried in a liquid; transported throughout the body by the circulatory system

brain: organ that is the control center for actions, thoughts, and emotions

C

carbohydrate: molecule made up of carbon, hydrogen, and oxygen, which is the product of photosynthesis; sugars and starches are examples

cardiac muscle: heart muscle; it is involuntary (not consciously controlled) and keeps the heart beating.

carnivore: an animal that feeds on other animals, such as a wolf

cell: basic unit of structure and function in living things

cell division: process by which cells divide to form new cells

cell membrane: structure that surrounds the cytoplasm of the cell

cellular respiration: process in cells by which oxygen is chemically combined with food molecules and energy is released

chemical equation: a way of writing changes in the arrangement of atoms during a chemical reaction, using chemical symbols

chemical reaction: change that takes place when two or more substances (reactants) interact to form new substances (products)

chlorophyll: green pigment in plants that captures the energy of sunlight for use in photosynthesis

chloroplast: a structure in a plant cell that contains chlorophyll; Sugar molecules are made in chloroplasts through the process of photosynthesis.

chromosome: the structure located in the nucleus of a cell, made of DNA, that contains the genetic information needed to carry out cell functions and make new cells

circulatory system: organ system that transports needed substances throughout the body and carries away wastes

class: division of organism classification below phylum and above order, as in the class *Insecta* (insects)

classify: to organize into groups based on similar characteristics

climate: the general pattern of weather over a long period of time

commensalism: relationship between species in which one species is helped and the other is unaffected

community: all of the populations sharing a specific area or region; for example, all the organisms in a lake

competition: in an ecosystem, occurs when more than one individual or population tries to make use of the same limited resource

conservation: the wise use and protection of natural resources

conservationist: person who protects endangered species and their habitats

continent: any of Earth's seven large land masses

control: factor in an experiment that is kept the same

convergent evolution: an evolutionary pattern in which unrelated species become more similar in order to survive in similar environmental conditions

culturing: growing living cells or tiny organisms in a protected environment with nutrients

cytoplasm: gel-like fluid that takes up most of the space inside a cell

D

data: collected information; the results of an experiment or other investigation

deforestation: destruction of the forest

desert: dry climate that receives an average of less than 25 cm of rainfall per year

dichotomous key: a system used for identifying plants, animals, rocks, or minerals, that is made up of a series of paired descriptions to choose between

digestion: process of breaking down food into a form the body can use

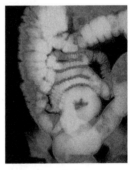

digestive system: organ system that breaks down food into substances the body can use and absorbs these substances

DNA: deoxyribonucleic acid; the material found in a cell's nucleus that determines the genetic traits of the organism

domain: the broadest category in the system used to classify every known organism on Earth

dominant: in a pair of genes, the form that, if present, determines the trait

E

echolocation: a system of using bounced sounds to determine the location of objects

ecology: study of interactions of organisms with each other and their environment

ecosystem: all the living populations in an area along with the nonliving parts of that environment

egg: female sex cell; also an object that contains an animal developing from a fertilized sex cell (such as a bird egg or insect egg)

electric current: the amount of electric charge that moves past a certain point each second; measured in amperes (A)

electricity: general term for interaction of electric charges

endangered species: a species that is in danger of extinction

endocrine system: system of organs that controls body activities through chemical messengers (hormones)

endoplasmic reticulum: structure in a cell that is involved in making proteins and transporting materials

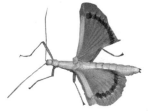

energy: ability to do work

entomology: the science of studying insects

environment: surroundings and conditions in which an organism lives

enzyme: a protein in the body that helps control a chemical reaction, such as digestion

epidemic: an outbreak of a disease that affects many people

epithelial stem cells: cells from an adult's skin that can specialize into different kinds of cells

evolution: theory, based on scientific evidence, that describes how species change over many generations

experiment: series of steps that, under controlled conditions, produces data that test a hypothesis or prediction

extinct: condition in which there are no more living members of a species

F

family: division of organism classification below order and above genus, as in *Felidae* (cats)

fat: kind of organic compound that makes up part of a cell membrane, stores excess food energy for an organism, helps insulate an organism, and has many other roles

feces: solid waste eliminated by the body

fertilization: union of a sperm cell with an egg cell

fetus: a developing mammal from the time its major organs are formed until birth; in humans, this is from 8 weeks to about 40 weeks

food chain: in an ecosystem, path of food energy from the sun to a producer to a series of consumers

food web: in an ecosystem, arrangement of several overlapping food chains

force: a push or a pull

fossil: remains, impressions, tracks, or other evidence of ancient organisms

free-fall: a falling motion that is affected only by gravity, not by a parachute or other object

frequency: number of wave vibrations (oscillations) produced in one second, measured in hertz (Hz)

fungi: single or many-celled organisms that have cells walls, do not have chlorophyll, take food from the environment, and reproduce by budding or by spores

G

gene: segment of DNA, found on a chromosome, that determines the inheritance of a particular trait

generation: one set of offspring

genome: all the genes that an organism has

genus: division of organism classification below family and above species, as in *Felis* (the genus that includes house cats); *See also scientific name*

gills: organs that absorb oxygen in water

glands: specialized organs that make substances (hormones) that control and regulate body processes

glucose: simple sugar made by plants through the process of photosynthesis

Golgi apparatus: cell structure that helps package and distribute products within the cell

grassland: large land region in which the main types of plants are grasses

gravity: force of attraction between any two objects

H

habitat: the place in an ecosystem where an organism lives

heart: organ in the circulatory system that pumps blood throughout the body

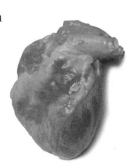

herbicide: chemical used to kill unwanted plants

herbivore: animal that feeds only on plants, such as a deer

horizontal axis: a horizontal line marked with a scale that is used to place data points on a graph; sometimes called the x-axis

hormone: a chemical released by a gland; controls a specific body function

hydroelectric power: electricity that is generated by using the energy of moving water

hyperthyroidism: a condition in which the thyroid gland produces too much of its hormone

hypothesis: an idea that can be tested by experiment or observation

I

immune system: system that protects the body against disease

infectious: capable of spreading disease

inference: an explanation that is based on available evidence but is not a direct observation

intestines: See *large intestine, small intestine*

ion: atom or molecule that has an overall electric charge due to loss or gain of electrons

J

joint: place where two or more bones meet

K

kingdom: largest grouping in organism classification, as in the animal kingdom

Glossary of Scientific Terms

L

large intestine: part of the digestive system where water is absorbed from solid waste

life cycle: all stages in the life of an organism

liver: organ in the digestive system that produces bile and enzymes, breaks down toxins and wastes, and has many other functions

lungs: pair of organs in the respiratory system, where carbon dioxide and oxygen are exchanged

M

mammal: animal that has fur or hair, usually gives birth to live young, and can nurse its young with milk

mass: amount of matter in something; measured in grams (g)

metabolism: cellular processes of making, storing, and transporting chemicals; also, the sum of all these processes in an organism

microscopic: object or organism too small to be seen without a microscope

migration: seasonal movement of animals from one place to another

mitochondria: structures in the cell that transform the energy in food into a form cells can use to carry out their activities

model: simplified version of some part of the natural world that helps explain how it functions

molecule: smallest particle of a substance that still has the properties of that substance

mutation: a random change in a gene

mutualism: relationship between two species in which both species benefit

N

natural selection: process by which organisms change over time as those with traits best suited to an environment pass their traits to the next generation

nectar: sweet liquid found in some flowers

niche: role that a species plays in a living community or ecosystem

nucleus: structure near the center of a cell that contains the cell's DNA

nutrient: substance that an organism needs in order to survive and grow

O

order: division of organism classification below class and above family, as in the order *Carnivora* (mammals that feed on other animals)

organ: in an organism, structure made of two or more different tissues that has a specialized function; for example, the lungs

organelles: structures in the cytoplasm of a cell that carry out cell activities

organism: a living thing

organ system: group of organs that work together to do a specific job for an organism, such as the digestive system

osmosis: diffusion of water across a membrane, such as a cell membrane

ovary: female sex organ in which egg cells are produced

P

pancreas: organ of the digestive system and endocrine system; makes enzymes that help in the breakdown of carbohydrates and that help regulate blood sugar levels

parasitism: relationship between species in which one species (parasite) benefits and the other (host) is harmed but not usually killed

photosynthesis: chemical process by which plants use light energy to make glucose from water and carbon dioxide

phylum: first division of organism classification below kingdom, as in the phylum *Arthropoda*

pollen: particles that carry male genetic material, from seed plants

pollination: the transfer of pollen from the male part of a plant (stamen) to the female part (pistil)

population: all the members of a species living in a particular area at a particular time

predator: animal, such as a lion, that kills and eats other animals (prey)

prediction: a guess about what will happen under certain conditions, based on observation and research

prey: organism that is killed and eaten by another organism (predator)

producer: organism that makes its own food, such as a plant or a photosynthetic alga

proteins: organic compounds that make up living things and are essential for life

protists: one-celled or simple many-celled organisms, such as amoebas and algae

R

recessive: in a pair of genes, the form that is masked if a dominant form is present

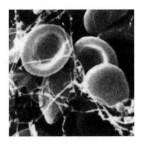

red blood cell: cell that carries oxygen through the body

reflex: an animal's automatic response to a stimulus, such as jerking away from a hot surface

reproduce: to make more individuals of the same species from a parent organism or organisms

respiration: See *cellular respiration*

ribosome: structure in a cell where proteins are put together

S

satellite: object that revolves around a larger object in space; The moon is a natural satellite of Earth; the Hubble Space Telescope is an artificial satellite.

scientific name: the genus and species name of an organism; for example, *Aplodontia rufa*, mountain beaver

seed: structure able to sprout and develop into a plant; made of a plant embryo and its food supply

sense organs: organs that gather information about the surrounding environment, including the eyes, ears, nose, mouth, and skin

skeletal muscle: muscle that moves parts of the body and is under conscious control of the organism

Glossary of Scientific Terms

small intestine: organ in the digestive system that completes digestion and absorbs nutrients

smooth muscle: muscle, found in many organs, that is not under conscious control of the organism

sound: energy that travels through matter as mechanical waves and can be heard by the ear

species: group of organisms that can mate and produce offspring that in turn can produce more offspring; also, most specific division of organism classification, below genus; *See also scientific name*

sperm: male sex cell, produced in the testes

spinal cord: bundle of nerves that goes from the brain stem down the center of the backbone

stomach: organ in the digestive system where food is stored and partially digested before it enters the small intestine

stomata: tiny openings in plant leaves that take in carbon dioxide and release oxygen

symbiosis: a close relationship between two species

T

tendon: connective tissue that attaches skeletal muscle to bone

thyroid gland: gland that functions in making hormones that control chemical processes in the body

tissue: in plants and animals, a group of cells that work together to do a specific job

trait: an inherited characteristic of an organism

tumor: a growth of cells that is not normal

V

variable: In experiments: a condition that is changed in order to find out the effect of that change

venom: a poisonous substance released by an animal

vertical axis: a vertical line marked with a scale that is used to place data points on a graph; sometimes called the y-axis

W

watt (W): unit of power, equal to one joule per second (1 J/s)

wildlife preserve: special area set aside as a habitat for wild animals and plants; also called wildlife sanctuary

Z

zoology: the science of studying, observing, and classifying animals